DECIDE TO LOVE

A BIBLICAL GUIDE TO CHRISTIAN LIVING

Anthony L. Ash

 BOOKS

An SPC Publication
Fort Worth, Texas 76137

A complete *Teacher's Manual/Resource Kit* for use with this paperback is available from your religious bookstore or the publisher.

DECIDE TO LOVE
Copyright © 1980 by Sweet Publishing Company,
Fort Worth, Texas 76137

Unless otherwise indicated, scripture quotations are from the Revised Standard Version of the Bible, copyrighted in 1946, 1952, and 1971 by the Division of Christian Education, National Council of Churches, and used by permission.

Edited by Garner Roberts and Byron Williamson
Cover designed by Charles Wallis, Inc.

Printed in the U.S.A.
Library of Congress Catalog Card Number 80-80294
ISBN 0-8344-0116-9
4 5

To My Parents

From Dad I learned "I did it because I love you."

It was Mom who would "read me with the Sing Book."

They taught me love, in its varied forms,

and thus undergirded and shielded my life.

Contents

PREFACE

I would like to think the opportunity to write this preface is providential. Books are written for various reasons. This one was written because I very much wanted to say some things to the church. I hope you will know how important it is to me to write these words, so that, as you read, you will consider them more important.

We may need to decide to love as much as we need anything. As I examine the personal and collective problems I have seen in the church for the past three decades, this impression is deepened daily. If we could love, everything else would follow. If I had one sermon to preach, or one line to write, it would be that we should *decide to love*. I cannot stress it enough. When I complete my life and look back to see what I have allowed God to accomplish through me, I hope I can say he has used me to encourage people to be more loving. I even hope I can say he has used this book—dare I say, powerfully—to that end.

That doesn't mean I am bragging about this volume. Authors are biased, and so I really can't say if what you are about to read is bad or good or in-between, in regard to style, organization, and the like. But I do know the subject matter is transcendent. God has given the topic, and I pray he will use it, whatever the failures of the human writer.

Some interesting events have led to the writing of these words. These events compose the complete picture of an emerging awareness of a need and a response to that need. Very early in my Christian experience I began to hear sermons on Christian unity. Early in my ministry, my own sermons echoed the appeal I heard from older preachers: let's unite on the basis of the Bible only.

That idea has not diminished in importance. But as I thought through the matter, it seemed that for people to agree intellectually on the central truths of the faith was not quite enough. People could believe the same doctrines, yet treat each other abominably. At this point I discovered the first three verses of Ephesians 4. There Paul's program for unity first calls for an attitude described variously as lowliness, meekness, patience, forbearance, peacefulness, and love. Apparently the common points of belief and experience mentioned in the next three verses of Ephesians are to be based on love. Love is a highly important part of the quest for oneness in Christianity.

Next I became concerned with the fractured state of the church. My early preaching experience came in the midst of a severe church split. It began in the mid-1950's, and its repercussions continue even today. Further, I was in the part of the country where the fighting was hottest. Preachers were pushed to declare themselves, and woe to the man who tarried or decided on neutrality. I observed the devilish results of such a division. Many years later I saw some of the same people, humbled by the passing of time, reaching out to be reconciled with their estranged brethren. "Why," I thought, "did all this happen? If love had prevailed in the beginning, it could have been avoided."

This does not diminish the importance of the "issues" (at least as viewed by the disputants). But, in my opinion, it was not the "issues" that were the real difficulty; it was *lovelessness*. This conclusion was reinforced in those rare instances when I saw brethren with strong differences maintaining a loving relationship, each party allowing the other the liberty of his convictions. Issues need not be divisive if love is in the camp. At least, not when the issues deal with matters peripheral to the faith. Even when the matters are central, men can love one another.

During my first year of full-time teaching I was conducting a class in the life and teachings of Jesus. As I thought through the ethical and moral teachings of the Lord, I began to wonder if they could be reduced to fewer and fewer items, and even eventually to one all embracing command, the proper keeping of which would actually lead to the keeping of all others. These ideas were passing through my mind, and I had formulated a dim answer when I asked one of my classes this question: "Is there a basic command given by Jesus which undergirds all others, and to which they can all be reduced?" A girl in the back raised her hand and replied, "I believe it would be love." Her conclusion matched and solidified mine. In the subsequent years, I have tested and refined this conclusion, and become fully convinced it is true. Love, *biblically defined*, is certainly the one attitude and mode of behavior from which all the rest must evolve.

I was still developing these ideas some four years later, when I was invited to an after-church social in the home of a well-known preacher. The conversation turned to the church. Presently the host inquired of each of us, "What is the greatest need in the church today?" That's a heavy question, and I pondered my answer as each of the others gave his. "It has to be love," I said when my turn came. "More than anything else we must love men—brothers and outsiders—as God loves us." Amen! With this, all else comes right.

These episodes give a psychological "flow sheet." Against such a background, my attention was called to the marvelous words of Paul in 1 Corinthians 13. This text became the basis for a sermon, then for a series of four sermons, and finally for a series of thirteen sermons. At length the text so captured me that I believed it had to be written. Thus, the book you now hold has grown and been refined over many years. May it bless your life.

So this is how I have proceeded. My first concern has been to know what Paul meant by each of the terms he used, in the context of the Corinthian situation. That explains the word analyses. Before we move to application, we must be sure we are applying the right thing. So I pondered these char-

10

acteristics, trying my best to comprehend the author's meaning.

Then there was the task of application. The practical sections of the chapters are as specific as possible, since generalizations are difficult to put into practice. Thus the attempt has been made to be personal, to get inside the human to consider what happens there when we love.

Finally, I want you, the reader, to be constantly aware of the help God gives us to become loving. Thus I have often spoken of prayer in these pages. This book was written with prayer, and it is hoped it will be read in the same manner. These words are aimed at changing lives. If they do, to God be the glory.

1 THE LOVE TEST

Why do we have so much trouble in the church? Why can't we treat each other better? I heard a man blow off steam for twenty minutes because he felt a Christian sister hadn't accepted his apology. Earlier I listened to the woman do the same thing because she felt the same man was ungrateful and unjustly critical. And this isn't an isolated case.

We give each other the "cold shoulder," gossip about each other, divide churches, and even lock each other out of church buildings. You can probably recall times when you shook your head in disbelief about such things. All of us have asked, "What can we do about it?"

I don't want to imply that everything about the church is this way. Many books could be written about good Christian relationships. But some things in our congregations need improving. We

13

have suffered from conflicts between Christians long enough!

There is help for us in the Bible. Early Christians had similar problems. In Paul's first letter to the church in Corinth, we learn that he faced problems as troubling as any we see today (maybe worse). In this book we will notice God's answers to some of these problems and how they relate to our own times.

Paul met these troubles head on with the power of God's love. One of the great passages in the New Testament is Paul's call to love in 1 Corinthians 13:1-7. He shows us that every problem can be worked out if we love each other. But we must first understand what love is, and we must make love a natural part of our lives.

The Love Answer

The love answer is always the right one. It will work today just as it did in Paul's time. It is important for us to discuss it, so I hope this book will help the church become what God wants her to be.

Paul knew love was the answer to the problems he encountered because he was an inspired man. He brought the Corinthians face to face with Jesus—the gift of God's love. His life continues to show men what love is about. He taught that God is love, and that those who follow Him must be loving too. But to really understand what Paul says, we must go past him and study Jesus.

A lawyer once came to Jesus and asked, "How can I find the way to eternal life?" Jesus said, "The first thing is to love God with all your being. Then, you are to love your neighbor as you love yourself" (Luke 10:25-28). We have no reason to question the importance of these two commandments. Jesus said all the law and prophets depended on them (Matt. 22:34-40), and he said no other commandment in the law is greater than these two (Mark 12:38-41).

Jesus wasn't saying anything new, for both love for God and love for man were also part of Jewish belief (Deut. 6:4; Lev. 19:18). But he gave them greater emphasis, and modeled their true meaning. It's easy to talk about such things without doing them.

First, how do we love God? We aren't loving him if we just try to manufacture holy feelings and call them love. Basically , we love God by revolutionizing our priorities. That means nothing should be more important than seeking God's kingdom (Matt. 6:33). To do this, we must first observe Jesus, who sought God's kingdom perfectly. We must be obedient to God's will. We must constantly try to put God in the very center of our hearts and let everything else revolve around the center.

I get fanatical about watching my favorite football team on TV. I behave as though nothing should get in the way—work, wife, meals, nothing. The game is absolute top priority, and any other activities take second place. So it should be with God if we love him above all. Nothing else can come before him.

Neighbor Love

Love for God is sometimes a hard thing to understand. That's when we consider the second great commandment. We best show our love for God when we love our neighbor. That's the lesson we learn from the story of the good Samaritan. Read Luke 10:25-37 carefully, and you will see that

15

the lawyer wanted to interpret the command to love his neighbor in a limited way. If he could limit the definition of neighbor, then he could love people who fit that definition, and not worry about loving anyone else.

We can guess who this Jew wanted to leave out of the "neighbor" category. Try Samaritans, tax collectors, and prostitutes for starters. Jesus didn't argue the point. Instead, he told about the good Samaritan, and said that loving your neighbor means loving anyone who needs your help. Do you think the lawyer saw his own attitudes reflected in the behavior of the priest and the Levite? How much impact has this story had on you?

Jesus teaches that we don't really love God unless we love our neighbor. And we don't truly love our neighbor if we don't aid him in his need. We all know people who are not attractive to us. But if we love them, we will do good for them. We easily love people who love us and are good to us. Then we feel we have loved our neighbor. Sure, we should love these nice people, but Jesus said even sinners do that (Luke 6:33, 34; Matt. 5:46, 47).

Jesus wants you to love people who aren't so nice. He wants you to love people who gripe and sneer and criticize and don't give you the time of day. He wants you to love people you don't even know. And as long as they need help, they are your neighbor (by Jesus' definition) and you are to love them.

Shocking Love

Most people can understand (at least in theory) loving God and loving neighbor. But imagine how it shocks them when he says, "Love your enemies" (Matt. 5:43-48; Luke 6:27-36). When you think about it, there isn't anyone you shouldn't love.

Love your enemy! Do good to those who hate you! Don't try to get even with people who have done you wrong! Be generous to people who rob you! Make the needs of other people (even the most repulsive) more important than your own material interests! Lend to those in need (even if they don't repay)! You can't escape it! When I think about a personal application of this lesson, it seems nearly impossible. I need a huge amount of God's help to love my enemies.

Jesus teaches us to love our enemies because God loves even his enemies (Matt. 5:43-48). God gives sun and rain to good and evil, just and unjust. He is kind to the ungrateful and selfish (Luke 6:35). You can't find a person, no matter how rotten, whom God doesn't love.

God loves the depressed and the silly, complainers and back-slappers, the faithful and unfaithful. He offers salvation to everyone! He loves people who don't want his love—who curse and reject him. God seeks the highest good for every man, no matter how wicked. No wonder Jesus, who reveals God's nature, taught us to love our enemies. He not only taught it, he did it.

Brother Love

What Jesus says here forms the basis for all later Christian teaching. Love God, love neighbor, love the enemy! To these he adds one more. Love your brethren (John 13:34). Although this is implied by what we have already said, we need to give it particular emphasis. Paul appealed to that special kind of love when he wrote the Corinthians. Christians are a part of a community—the church. The mark

17

of that community should be a love that shows the world that Christians have truly been changed by Christ.

Our love for each other is a sign that God sent Jesus (John 17:20-26). There is no doubt that the church is composed of people different from each other. The same social, economic, and philosophical things that divide people from one another outside the church also have the potential to divide the church. The difference? There should be so much love in the church that such difficulties are overcome. People who have received God's perfect love are able to love each other.

The Love Decision

What does this four letter word really mean? In the passages we have noticed, the Greek verb translated "to love" is *agapao*. The noun for love is *agape*. These terms refer to a resolution, to a making up of the mind.

Some folks think love is just a feeling—a warm, smiling, hugging sort of thing. We all like warmth and smiles and hugs. But that isn't the basic nature of agape love. The term indicates that we "make up our minds" to love, to seek the best for each man, to care. So when feelings come and go, this love remains because it is a mental decision.

Christian love acts a certain way, both when it feels good to act that way and when it doesn't.

We may get a better understanding of love by considering parents and children. Parents who really love their kids will seek their good. They will do this even when they don't like the way their children behave. Parents will do it even when they are angry and frustrated, and when warm emotional feelings toward their children are hard to come by. They will do it when the kids are sassy, or disobedient, or dirty and smelly.

I can remember times in my own youth when surely I was unlovable. In fact, I was so bad that Dad had to lay hands on me with what I considered to be catastrophic results. Then after we had shared in a disciplinary experience, he would tell me, "I did that because I love you." I know now (although I doubted it then) that he was telling me the truth. To me, his love was certainly not of the "warm feeling" kind. The only warm feeling was on the seat of my pants.

Love is at the very heart of Jesus' teaching. If Christians are ever supposed to be anything, they are to be loving. This is the very nature of God. An unloving follower of the infinitely loving God is a spiritual freak. So, a church which lacks love needs to be called back to its basic nature and purpose. Paul saw a church like this in Corinth. So he referred to the Lord's life and teaching—to the very root of what Christian life is supposed to be—and found the answer to the Corinthians' problems. And he gives us answers to our problems also. Christianity stays the same, and human needs stay the same, and certainly God is the same.

The Trouble with Love

If you skim 1 Corinthians you will find enough church problems to give any preacher or church leader a splitting headache. The Corinthians were immoral, unspiritual, jealous, stuck-up, and selfish. They were divided into competitive parties. Their homes were in real trouble, and so was their worship in the assembly. Some of them had totally bogus views of important Christian truths. We get the impression they were only "playing church."

19

In chapter 12 Paul talks about spiritual gifts. God had given different people different gifts (verses 8-11), and it was entirely his business what gift he gave to whom. He intended for the church to be like a human body, with each part serving its purpose. An eye is not a right hand, but you need them both. Still, God's generous gifts didn't suit all the Corinthians. Some sulked because of gifts they didn't have and others did. And others became arrogant because they thought their gifts put them above the rest. Arrogance and envy! And the body was breaking down, like someone afflicted by cancer, cerebral palsy, and a mental breakdown all at the same time.

Paul faced the problem head on, and said at the end of chapter 12, "I will show you a still more excellent way." And that is where he confronts us all with what Jesus said and showed earlier about love. Paul here breaks love down into its component parts. Like light refracted through a prism, the result is a powerful statement:

1 Corinthians 13:1-7

If I speak in the tongues of men and of angels, but have not love, I am a noisy gong or a clanging cymbal. And if I have prophetic powers, and understand all mysteries and all knowledge, and if I have all faith, so as to remove mountains, but have not love, I am nothing. If I give away all I have, and if I deliver my body to be burned, but have not love, I gain nothing.

Love is patient and kind; love is not jealous or boastful; it is not arrogant or rude. Love does not insist on its own way; it is not irritable or resentful; it does not rejoice at wrong, but rejoices in the right. Love bears all things, believes all things, hopes all things, endures all things.

We'll spend most of this book talking about those parts of love described in verses 4-7 (the last paragraph of the quotation). But let's look now at the first paragraph (verses 1-3). Read that several times. Pretty radical, isn't it? We could have some or all of those talents and gifts, but without love we would be absolute spiritual zeros. It seems almost impossible that what Paul says can be true. But it is. And when we get over the shock of his words it dawns on us—"This love business is *really* important."

If you still haven't gotten the message, think how Paul might have written these words to us. We don't want to be negative and judgmental, but there are lots of ways we consider people as really important in the church. Like a well-known preacher, or a highly regarded educator, or a well-trained scholar, or an influential writer, or a famous debator, and so on. Paul might say of such people, and others, "Even with all this you are nothing—if you don't have love!" That would raise some eyebrows. But, we would have to agree that Paul was right.

The Love Test

Turn it around. People you have never heard of may be the greatest Christians in the world, when judged by the love test. I know a widow whose name you have never heard. Her loving deeds would fill this book. I think of an elder in a small church in an out-of-the way place who has to rank way up on God's list because he continually shows so much love to everyone. Gifts, visits, kind words, sacrifices, and caring—love in many forms.

21

And where you find these things . . . there are the real saints. So says Paul. Or so he would say if he were here.

Some of you are probably having a guilt trip now because you know you aren't as loving as you should be. You may get that same reaction several times before you finish reading this book. I get the same feeling when I write about all this. That's why it is so terrific to know that God never asks of us anything he won't help us do.

Paul told the Corinthians, and us, about an ideal. It's an ideal none of us has yet perfectly achieved. God knows that. He is pleased with the efforts we make. But, it is more important to know he will transform us into loving people. To be loving is not a goal we achieve by ourselves. Divine power leads and molds us into the very nature of God—love. We reach out and claim God's strength. And he gives it (Rom. 5:5). He changes our attitudes and our actions. I am so relieved that it doesn't depend just on my own power because I know how often and how inevitably I goof up.

So, a lot of prayer is in order. We will return to this need again and again in these pages. God plans for us to have victorious growth within ourselves and in our relationships with each other. The future for people surrendered to God is bright. We hope that this book will help us claim God's power.

2^{THE} PATIENCE PRESCRIPTION

Do you know Roy G. Biv? Probably not, unless you used the same method to memorize the colors of the spectrum I did when I was in junior high school. The letters in Roy G. Biv reminded me of the colors red, orange, yellow, green, blue, indigo, and violet. In the first chapter we said Paul was doing a "Roy G. Biv" with love in 1 Corinthians 13:4-7. He explains love by dividing it into parts. Although love has more facets, the principle is the same. By dividing love into its recognizable traits, he makes the idea hit home more forcefully. It's often easy to sidestep the word love because it is so general, but it's harder for me to get around the need for patience, especially after a trying business meeting.

The first quality of love Paul mentions is patience. But there is something else. What Paul said in 1 Corinthians 13:1-7 about the importance of love applies equally to the various exhibitions of love. Get the point? To put it more directly, he is saying that without patience (since love is patient), we are *nothing* (faith and knowledge and tongues notwithstanding).

Often when I think of patience, or impatience, I remember how frustrated I get when some piece of machinery breaks down (my car, the washing machine, the garbage disposal, and so on). Sometimes I want to take a baseball bat and bash the offender because the inconvenience is going to cost me time and money. You can probably understand my feelings. Paul wasn't talking about things like that (whatever the first century equivalents might have been). His words make sense only if we realize he was talking about patience with people. So get mad at your dead battery if you want, but don't lose patience with your "dead" brothers the same way.

An Impatient Church

If you don't understand why he was talking about patience, remember the kind of church Paul was addressing. Remember the problems, like divisions over preachers, carnality, lawsuits, and even dissension in worship. Imagine what it would be like in that congregation. Gossip, temper tantrums, suspicion, side-choosing, bad feelings, and other ugly things. You may know of a church today with similar problems. A large dose of Christian patience was urgently needed in the church in Corinth.

Let's examine the nature of the medicine Paul prescribed. Word studies aren't always exciting, but they usually help us better understand an idea. In the original Greek New Testament in 1 Corinthians 13:4, you will find the word *makrothumei*. If you examine the other places in the New Testament which use the same family of words, you will find ten uses of the verb, fourteen uses of the noun, and one other related form. In the King James they are translated with the basic meanings of "longsuffering," "patient," or "steadfast." (The passages are Matt. 18:26, 29; Luke 18:7; Acts 26:3; Rom. 2:4; 9:22; 1 Cor. 13:4; 2 Cor. 6:6; Gal. 5:22; Eph. 4:2; Col. 1:11; 3:12; 1 Thess. 5:14; 1 Tim. 1:16; 2 Tim. 3:10; 4:2; Heb. 6:12, 15; James 5:7 (2), 8, 10; 1 Pet. 3:20; 2 Pet. 3:9, 15).

In the first chapter we stressed the idea that love is God's nature. The call to love is a call to be like God. If you decide from this that patience is before all else a characteristic of God, you are right. As we examine these passages, that has to be our first conclusion. Before it describes anything else, patience describes God. As a matter of fact, he is the one who gives the word meaning.

An Incentive for Patience

The Bible says God's patience with mankind is the reason he overlooked human stubbornness and perfected the plan of redemption. That is why Christians regard the patience of the Lord to be salvation (2 Pet. 3:15). Because God is patient, he gives men chances to repent. Furthermore, he gives them strong incentives to repent (Rom. 2:4; 9:22). Peter sees an example of God's long-suffering in Noah (1 Pet. 3:20). Behind Paul's burning zeal for Christ lay his very deep appreciation for God's patience. He felt it personally because he knew he had been the "chief of sinners." Yet God waited for him to change and redeemed him. Paul realized that if a scoundrel like himself could be saved through God's patience, then salvation was available for anyone (1 Tim. 1:16).

Peter also says it powerfully and beautifully, "The Lord is not slow about his promise as some count slowness, but is forbearing toward you, not wishing that any should perish, but that all should reach repentance" (2 Pet. 3:9). By now, people who realize how wonderful it is to be saved by God's patience probably feel like shouting, "Praise the Lord."

Ten Million Dollar Patience

In Matthew 18:23-35, Jesus tells a powerful story about the patience of God. It is about a servant who owed a huge debt. He begged patience (verse 26) from his creditor, and, incredibly enough, was forgiven the whole amount. If that doesn't impress you, then consider that he owed, by our standards, at least $10,000,000. In fact, with inflation, this amount is probably too low. Also, he lived in a time when the average wage probably wasn't much more than twenty cents a day. Jesus was talking about how great God's love for man (and patience with man) is, but his illustration is almost beyond our imagination.

In Romans 1 we get another form of the same thing. It tells of the terrible immorality and ungodliness of the Gentiles (verses 20-32). But God bears with all that, still hoping men will be saved (Rom. 2:4). That's pretty impressive!

This wonderful patience came to earth and appeared where men could see it in the person of Jesus. His love for men was so great that he endured insult after insult and held on through the crucifixion so men might be saved.

That's pretty hard for us to understand. Yes, we

know something about patience. "But this thing has a limit," we think. "After all, we can only be patient so long." But our outlook is far short of God's infinite long-suffering. When we would be crying out for judgment on sinners, God is still saying, "Wait, maybe they will yet repent."

God is love. God's love is patient. Love is patient. Christians who love are patient. Other New Testament passages also encourage patience. It is part of the fruit of the Spirit (Gal. 5:22). It is to be put on by those redeemed in Christ (Col. 3:12). The great statement on church unity in Ephesians 4:2 makes it clear that we can't reach oneness in Christ unless we are patient.

A Patient Faith

James and the author of Hebrews give us more examples of patience. The book of Hebrews makes a long argument addressed to discouraged Christians (see 6:12-15). Like we sometimes are, they were tempted to quit Christianity. They wanted to go back to what they believed were the comforts of Moses and their Jewish background. The author uses a lot of ways to encourage them, but in this passage he asks them to consider Abraham, a man "who through faith and patience" received the inheritance God promised.

Abraham could have chucked the whole series of promises God made to him. God told him his descendants would have a land, and all Abraham ever owned was a burial plot. God told him he would have numerous descendants, but he and his wife were too old to have their own children. Then, when a child, Isaac, was born by God's miraculous power, God told Abraham to kill him as a sacrifice (Gen. 22). If he had seen things the way men today usually see things, do you think Abraham would have continued to trust God? I doubt it. But Abraham let God's promises become the biggest things in his life. He hung on to them for dear life, through thick and thin, with incredible patience, and even when people could have said it was nonsense to do so. Finally, God's word came true, as it always does. To us, Abraham is the father of the faithful because he had such a patient faith.

Abraham's patience was not the patience with people that Paul talks about in 1 Corinthians 13. But both kinds have the same quality. Both maintain a conviction and a manner of life because of what the patient person believes to be true. So whether we are patient with people or with life's circumstances, the attitude of staying power is the same. The writer of Hebrews was telling people not to give up on Christ. And Paul was telling people not to give up on Christ by not giving up on other people.

Staying Power

James doesn't talk about patience with people, either (5:7-11). But he talks about the same staying power we need in being patient with people. James writes to people who are tired of awaiting the Lord's return. They are tempted to take a limited view of life and center their lives in the satisfactions wealth brings. James tells them (5:1-6) that such a goal is a loser, and it will finally bring misery. Since he doesn't want his readers to make that mistake, he urges them to keep their faith, without complaining, in spite of any difficulties.

Then James gives his readers some help with an illustration. First, think about a farmer. He has to wait patiently through the growing season till his crop matures. Impatient people who want their profit "now" could never make it farming. James' readers could see the point. Some good things come only for those who wait and work. Don't give up in the early summer. The crop is coming. And don't give up on Jesus, because he is coming again.

For a second witness (or group of witnesses) of patience, James introduces the prophets, men of extraordinary courage. They had their lives centered in God and in the declaration of his message. They refused to be pressured into compromising. Their vision centered on man's need for God, and they burst through all barriers to speak his word.

But it was often difficult for the prophet. Many times they might have given up. But God's grasp on them would not let them. Elijah had times of deep despair, as in the episode at Horeb (1 Kings 19:18). He thought he stood all alone as a spokesman for the Lord. Yet he was reassured by the still small voice of faith that there were others who had not bowed the knee to Baal. So he kept going.

Isaiah preached for more than 50 years, even though in the very beginning, at his call, God told him people would resist his message (Isa. 6:9f.). But he had the vision of what God wanted, and didn't give up on it.

Jeremiah, who preached nearly as long as Isaiah, is called the weeping prophet. He was timid and sensitive, and went through a whole parade of troubles because of his preaching. He wasn't a popular preacher. And how he struggled under the burden (Jer. 11:18-12:6; 15:10-21; 17:14-18; 18:18-23; 20:7-18). But he kept at it because the message burned within him and would not let him stop (20:9).

Ezekiel, Jeremiah's contemporary, faced such hardheaded opposition God told him his forehead would have to be made harder than those of the people who heard him (Ezek. 3:8f.).

James says the prophets kept to the task no matter what, just as Christians steadfastly await the Lord's return. Paul says we should have the same staying power with people.

Job, the steadfast, is James' third illustration. Job complained a lot (who wouldn't, in his sandals). But he never quit believing in God, even when he blamed God for his suffering. Read Job and see how he maintained his faith.

These examples in James deal with the patience people had because of their conviction about God. We're discussing patience toward people, but we do it also because of our convictions about God, and what he has done for us through Jesus.

Love Is Patient

When Paul spoke about his ministry in Corinth, he described patience as one of its characteristics (2 Cor. 6:6). We can certainly understand why. His behavior makes his words "love is patient" more powerful. He wrote his protege, Timothy, and told him he would have to be patient in his convincing, rebuking, and exhortation (2 Tim. 4:2). This was great counsel, and Paul reminded Timothy he had followed his own advice (2 Tim. 3:10).

Preachers, teachers, and parents need to remember God loves people and wants them changed, even if it takes a lifetime to do it and even if the change is small. We can't afford to blow this by temper tantrums or by giving up in disgust. We can't "fly off the handle" if our schemes for doing things aren't accepted. We have to be careful that we don't continually tell people off. We shouldn't get mad at people who disagree with us. We need to remember that it is easy to get "out of joint" when our egos are bruised.

We ask, "What is the greatest good I can do for people over a whole lifetime?" We all need to be patient with everyone, and for the same reason. God has been patient with us, so we are saved. We must be patient with others to help them know God's salvation.

We should be patient with church leaders whom we feel are stifling rather than promoting the growth of the church. We should be patient with our wives even when they can't stop charging more at the department store than the budget allows (though being patient doesn't rule out insisting less money be spent). We should be patient with husbands who spend most of the weekend watching sports on TV (though being patient doesn't rule out insisting less time be spent in front of the tube). We should be patient with people at work who are always riding us, even if they have no good reason. We should be patient with bigots and bullies and people who are "always right," and the stubborn and people with insulting tongues. Parents should be patient with kids who seem like they won't ever grow up. We could continue this list. Each of us could add those special cases that irritate us and make us want to give up.

Guilt and Impatience

In the first chapter we talked about feeling guilty because we aren't what we ought to be. I'm not trying to make anyone feel guilty. We can find the strength to be patient with the people around us. The first thing that will help is the right frame of mind. The more we center our thoughts on God's patience for us, the more that knowledge will change our lives. Sure there will be failures, probably up to the last day we live. I may get upset because my nurse doesn't answer the call button soon enough. But the more we think patience, the more that inner core of self will change and the outer actions will come into line. God's nature is inexhaustible patience with sinful humans. We must try to enter into the heart of God and share this divine attitude.

We are impatient when we think of ourselves more than of others. I get mad with my wife because she doesn't hear what I say, so she asks me the same question again five minutes later. But I ought to get over my self-centeredness and ask myself what need of hers I need to fill. Maybe if I were more communicative she would hear much better. But when we get stuck on our egos we will become angry or defensive or retaliatory—anything but patient. The more fully we learn from Jesus the concept of self-giving, the more patient we will become.

The second thing we can do is pray for God to help us. Help us recognize our faults. Help us know just what patience involves. Help us take the long-range view. We will be surprised at what God will do in our lives. "Did you hear? He's overcome his temper!" "He doesn't pop off like he used to!" "He has learned to suffer fools gladly!"

3 THE KINDNESS VACUUM

Another color Paul shows us in the love spectrum is kindness. When I think of kindness, and its opposite, I remember a story a friend told me. He was having a disagreement with his landlady over the rent. She was wrong, but no amount of talking seemed to change her mind. Finally, my friend appealed to her compassion and human feeling. She said she wasn't concerned about compassion and human feeling. In effect, she said, "The only interest I have in you is as a source of income." She was playing by different rules. She didn't care if they had a loving relationship or not. As far as she was concerned, it was pure business.

It destroys me when I am unkind to others. It also destroys me when others are unkind to me. Unkindness wrecks lives. An unkind husband destroys his wife. He criticizes her constantly about everything from cooking to housework to personal habits. She puts up with it until she can stand no more. Finally, she leaves him, in tears, and the next day sees a lawyer about divorce. The experience shatters her life. A couple gets tired of a steady diet of unsympathetic condemnation in their local congregation. They finally react to the unkindnesses by going elsewhere, or perhaps they just stop going to church. A teenager cries uncontrollably in her room because she has been the butt of unkind treatment from classmates. We see tragedies like these almost every day.

Kindness: Love in Action

What is kindness? The adjective form means "good, gracious, kind." The noun form means man's "goodness of heart, kindness." The basic meaning is goodness in action, with particular stress on qualities like good will, tenderness, compassion, sympathy, and considerateness. It can be a genuine compliment given to a family member, or fellow worker. It can be a note expressing appreciation. It can be the spirit of understanding when someone else makes a mistake, like when we say, "Don't worry. We all goof up."

Like patience, love is a word describing God. Love and patience in our lives are fragments of the divine life within us. The same thing is true of kindness. The terms the New Testament uses for kindness refer to the nature of God. Not just God in himself, but God in his dealings with men. Six passages illustrate this (Luke 6:35; Rom 2:4; 11:22; Eph. 2:7; Tit. 3:4; 1 Pet. 2:3).

A follower of Jesus should love his enemies, do good, and lend—expecting nothing in return. We should be that way because God is that way. He is kind (even) to the ungrateful and selfish (Luke 6:35).

We noted that God's patience is why men are redeemed and not destroyed. That passage (Rom. 2:4) also says God's rich kindness is the reason he continues to invite men to repent. Later in Romans (11:22) Paul discusses the salvation of the Gentiles. They too are to be saved by divine kindness. Though they are alien branches, God grafts them into the olive tree (Israel).

Paul gives another beautiful description of God's gift of redemption in Ephesians 2:1-10. Verse seven shows us the future with the measureless riches God is yet to give. In Titus 3:4, Paul speaks of the kindness of God, our Savior, and dramatically describes how the Lord overlooks man's wickedness (verse 3).

In 1 Peter 2:3, Paul says God's kindness is the power that has allowed Christians to be born anew to a living hope (1:3), which is an inheritance imperishable, undefiled, and unfading (1:4). It has opened the door to salvation (1:5), unutterable and exalted joy (1:8), freedom from futility (1:18), and purification (1:22).

Motivating Kindness

Each of these six scriptures describes kindness as the reason God makes our salvation possible. When someone does us a great favor, thankfulness for that favor motivates us. Years ago, while on an outing with my wife and her family, I foolishly tried to swim out to a ski jump in the middle of the lake. I am not a strong swimmer, and after I "stopped to rest," I found out I didn't have the energy to continue. I began to drown. Even today, years later, the memory terrifies me. Just before I went down the third time the young daughter of a friend heard my cries and threw a life preserver to me. She saved my life. If she hadn't responded, I wouldn't be writing this page now. She is now married, with children of her own. But my gratitude for what she did has not dimmed. If I can ever help her or her family I am willing to go far out of my way to do so because she has a special claim on my gratitude.

If I am grateful to a girl who saved me from drowning, men should show ultimate gratitude to God, who saved them from perdition. Each of these passages describing God's kindness calls upon people to respond. In Luke 6:35, Jesus mentions God's kindness to evil men to show why his followers should love even their enemies. In Romans 2:4, kindness leads men to repent and also admonishes Christians not to judge others. Romans 11:22 calls upon the reader to "keep the faith"—that is, continue in God's kindness and not fall away. The description of God's kindness in Ephesians 2:7 is a key part of an argument which leads to the ethical demands of chapters 4-6. Titus 3:4 shows kindness as the motive to practice good deeds, avoid stupid controversies, respect authority, avoid quarreling, speak evil of no one, and be gentle (Tit. 3:1-11). Finally 1 Peter 2:3 exhorts Christians to put away malice, guile, insincerity, envy and slander.

Not all of these qualities fall under the heading of kindness. But they all fall under the heading of grateful response for what God has done. It is easy to see how God's kindness leads Paul to tell us that we, as lovers, should be kind as well. I owe much to the girl who saved my life, to my parents, to my wife, and to the man who gave me $100 years ago when I was broke, but none of these things compare to what God has given me. He gives all, and even their gifts ultimately came from him. So if ever there was motive for anything, there is motive for me to have love—expressed in kindness. Clearly, kindness as part of the fruit of the Spirit (Gal. 5:22), leads to a pair of observations.

Unnatural Love

First, Christian kindness doesn't come naturally, according to Paul (Rom. 3:12). He describes human sinfulness with some Old Testament passages. One says, "there is none that does good." "Good" is the same word rendered "kind" elsewhere. Apparently, kindness (goodness) is often opposed to man's natural tendencies. We practice it now and then, but we are too selfish to make it a way of life. To be kind like God is kind, we need to be transformed. And that is what God does for us.

The second observation, then, is that when God changes us by his Spirit, kindness is part of the Spirit's fruit. It is a "supernatural" virtue, not a natural one. God will help me obey the obligation that "love is kind" places upon me. A better way to say this is that God will change me, if I will let him, into a kind person. I must want to try to change, but the outcome is the result of God's work.

Before we look at some applications of kindness, there are two other things that need to be said here.

Confronting Kindness

First, C. S. Lewis says there is no doubt that we need kindness. But he fears we have tried to reduce all virtue to kindness. We overlook matters like justice, commitment to principle, discipline and exhortation. For example, we should not let being kind blind us to the fact some things are simply not right. It is wrong for a man to indiscriminately divorce his wife and marry another woman whom he finds more attractive. Perhaps in our kindness we might be inclined to shy away from confronting him. But real love says, "You are wrong!" This needs to be done for the man's own good. If your neighbor, who hates animals, throws a piece of poisoned meat over the fence to your dog, you ought to confront that person. To use "kindness" as an excuse to avoid confronting him is less loving, not more. Your neighbor needs to face up to his deed for his own good.

The kindness Lewis warns against is a vague, convictionless desire to make everything pleasant for another person. But true kindness must occasionally require what seems unpleasant. When college students see a classmate cheating on a test, they are reluctant to tell the professor or to confront their classmate. They think it would be "unkind" to the cheater to get him in trouble or criticize him. But a person will be in more trouble going through life as a cheater than in being called to account for cheating during college. A habit of cheating will ruin his whole life, but an early confrontation gives him the chance to do better.

A parent may give in to a child's every whim because of mistaken kindness. But a parent who truly loves a child will not let the child eat only sweets, or get away with temper tantrums. If the best things are to be done for the child, parental kindness must be firm and tempered by other concerns.

This is not an either/or situation. We must not adopt an attitude of "anything goes so long as we are nice." Neither must we become sharp, abrasive, and unconcerned. We must be kind in all relations, but not sacrifice a greater principle by misunderstanding what kindness is.

The Kindness Vacuum

Second, if we can mistakenly make kindness the only virtue (and thus pervert its very nature), we can also overlook it completely. We sometimes let kindness slip by unnoticed and unpracticed. In concern for sound biblical teaching, do we forget to be kind and considerate to the person we think is wrong? We are told to oppose sin in the lives of other people, but sometimes we do it in inconsiderate ways.

We are often more concerned with saying to God, "There, I've done it," than to really help the sinner. Does the critical spirit sometimes show a lack of kindness? I know of places where someone is being "talked about" all the time. That may seem like fun to you when you are doing the talking. But what happens when you're not around, and then they talk about you? Isn't there some unkindness here? Little things, maybe. But little things make up lives. A lot of unkindness causes serious problems. A lot of kindness pays enormous dividends.

In my work, I often deal with divorced Christians. This includes editing a little monthly paper which we mail free to any who want it. You should read the letters of appreciation we get. The paper itself isn't much—four dinky pages per month. But the people who receive it are so desperate for help, for kindness, that even such a small thing becomes important. It breaks my heart to hear some of the stories they tell. There is no doubt in my mind of the Lord's wisdom when he bids us to be kind. People around us are crying out for kindness.

Kindness Is . . .

We are motivated by God's kindness to us, and we open our lives by prayer for God to help us be kind. A book describing all the ways to be kind would be too long. Not even God has given us that kind of book. But he gives us the basic principles. As you grow in Christ, you can figure it out for yourself. Do as the Lord did. That's the surest guide.

Perhaps a short list of "kind deeds" will stimulate your thoughts and actions. It is the right frame of mind, rather than the deeds themselves, which is the most important.

Kindness is the lady who makes fudge for the neighborhood children, then invites them to the feast with a spoon for each.

Kindness is visiting a hospital room with a genuine desire to minister to the patient there, whether by silence or by conversation.

Kindness is an executive, many years removed from his own rural beginning, who leaves his desk and drives twenty miles to a country farm to help an elderly brother, who is sick, with his plowing.

Kindness is a Christian druggist who greets his elderly customers at the door of his store because of his sincere concern for their well-being.

Kindness is someone who offers a cold drink to the yard man on a hot day.

Kindness is a friend who comes voluntarily in time of trouble seriously offering assistance.

Kindness is a person who tries to see good in others, rather than bad.

Kindness is a truck driver who stops to help a

stranded motorist fix a flat tire.

Kindness is a person who continues to be loving-ly concerned toward someone who refuses to be civil to him.

The Place to Start

Let's try another exercise. Based on what the Bible says, and your own insights, how would you apply loving kindness to each of the following cases?

. . . helping a couple with serious marital prob-lems.

. . . dealing with someone who has cheated you in business.

. . . dealing with someone who has just humil-iated you.

. . . dealing with someone you have just de-feated.

. . . relating to unqualified church leaders who are doing serious damage to the church.

. . . dealing with an incompetent minister if you are on the "hiring and firing" committee.

. . . dealing with someone who has repeatedly lied to you.

. . . responding to a person who calls you to repent from a smug, self-righteous attitude.

. . . dealing with someone you could easily, and truthfully, criticize.

The challenge is clear. God's response to our need is available. Let us open our hearts through prayer and let God show us how to be kind, loving people.

4 THE JEALOUS HEART

When someone does an outstanding thing or receives an honor, I smile and say, "That's really great!" But inside I wish it were me in their position. When some other person receives all the attention because of their reputation or wit, I think I ought to be the center of attention. People praise another preacher because of his sermons, and I choose, instead, to criticize him. Isn't all this really because I am jealous?

My problem is jealousy. It is in me and it is in you. It is in nearly everyone. So often it is covered up. We disguise it as "objective criticism," or opposition, or "He's a nice guy, but . . . " We like to camouflage our jealousy with objective analysis. Or we hide it by ignoring the person who is the object of attention. So when we come to "love is not jealous" we have a big problem on our hands.

Have I said anything that rings a bell and leads you to say, "Yes, I understand those feelings. I've had them myself"? If so, let's read 1 Corinthians 12 to help us understand what Paul was fighting. To get the background, read 1 Cor. 12:14-31. God had given special spiritual gifts to different Christians to be used for the good of the whole church. But they had been received and considered in the wrong spirit. Some people (verse 21) became arrogant about their gifts (we'll talk more about that in another chapter), but others felt they were of no use because their gifts were "inferior."

The folks with the "lesser" gifts may have become jealous of those with "greater" gifts. They had those same feelings I have sometimes. They handled it by saying, "Poor me. I don't matter." Paul answered, "But you *are* important. We are like a body in which all parts have significant places." He also said, "This is God's business. Why should we question him for giving gifts in the way he has?" And he reminded the brothers that love is not jealous.

If you have looked within yourself, as I have, and discovered jealousy, you should be concerned about ways to overcome it. So should I. But the better we understand the enemy, the more successfully we can fight him.

A Word on Jealousy

When you talk about something, it helps to know exactly what it means. So let's turn to the New Testament to find some other places where the word translated "jealousy" is used. The original word for jealousy, in both its noun and verb forms, is translated two different ways. And the two translations seem to be exact opposites—to be

44

contradictory. Many times the word is translated "zeal" (or an equivalent term). This is nearly always good. (Philippians 2:6 is an exception, and see also Hebrews 10:27, where the translation is "fury.") But in other scriptures the translation is "jealous," which is bad. How can this be?

Notice the places where the idea of zeal is found. Jesus had zeal for the temple (John 2:17), the Jews had a zeal for God (Rom. 10:2), and the Corinthians had a zeal for Paul (2 Cor. 7:7). There is a zeal produced by godly grief (2 Cor. 7:11) and a zeal in financial generosity (2 Cor. 9:2). Paul was zealous in persecuting the church (Phil. 3:6). These are all translations of the noun form of the word. The verb form describes an "earnest" search for spiritual gifts (1 Cor. 12:31; 14:1, 39).

The noun form of the same word translated jealousy (or an equivalent) is found twice in Acts (5:17; 13:45), several times in Paul's letters, and once in James. Jealousy is condemned in Romans 13:13; 1 Corinthians 3:3; 2 Corinthians 12:20, and Galatians 5:20. The verb is found in Acts 7:9; Acts 17:5; 1 Corinthians 13:4, and James 4:2.

This word study may be tedious, but it gets the evidence before us, and you can come back to it if you want to study the idea more closely.

Intense Concern

A close look at the passage shows a common element. They all suggest the idea of intense concern, so that the basic meaning of the original term is single-minded devotion. But people can be devoted to good things or bad. If the concern is channeled in the right direction, the usual translation of the Greek is zeal(with the exceptions noted above). Other translations could be ardor, eagerness, enthusiasm, and fervor. In fact, Jesus advocated we have this zeal when he called us to purity of heart (Matt. 5:8) and to having a single eye, full of light (Matt. 6:22).

But suppose this single-minded devotion should be turned the wrong way? Instead of being directed to God, what if it were turned toward material things, or to sensual excess? More to the point, suppose it were turned inward, making a person wholeheartedly devoted to self. This devotion to self causes jealousy. Anything other than myself poses a threat to my selfish ambition and becomes an object of jealousy. So jealousy, in its many forms, is a result of a fervent self-centeredness. This understanding of jealousy will help us conquer it.

A Jealous God

Remember that patience and kindness are attributes of God. By that logic, we might expect to say, "God is not jealous." But we remember that the Bible says God *is* a jealous God. For example, note 1 Corinthians 11:2, which says in the original, "I am jealous for you with a jealousy of God."

Jealousy is an intense devotion. God, by his very nature, is intensely devoted to himself, from all eternity. This sounds strange because we are speaking of God as if he were human. But if God eternally exists and is the Creator and Sustainer of all, then nothing else is really possible.

God's jealousy is not the peevish, anxious, irritable, capricious thing that human jealousy is. God's jealousy means God calls man to turn his life toward God. That is what men need. Nowhere else can we find real love, happiness, or peace. Nowhere else can we find life. God's jealousy

46

produces man's blessing. If you are jealous of me, and your jealousy is put into action, then I will likely be hurt. But divine jealousy is just the opposite. It is the source of all the good we need and want. God can only will our good. He will never hurt us by his jealousy. He calls us to be wholly dedicated to him, as he is to himself. (If he were not dedicated to himself, to what would he be dedicated?) God's jealousy is really God's love.

God wants us for himself. But when we are jealous, we turn away from him to ourselves. Through jealousy we make ourselves the most important thing. It makes a god of self. But intense devotion to self is not our greatest good. It is the barrier to obtaining our greatest good. It is the gateway to misery, leading to final destruction. It goes against the grain of what is best for man, for you and me.

Man's Jealousy

One writer reminds us that most of our jealousy pops up in one of two ways. First, we want to have as much as, or more than, the other person. Second, we want them to have as little as, or less than, we do. We try hard to keep up with the Joneses. Advertisers know how to manipulate our jealousy. They fuel our desire not only for things, but for more and better things than others have. And we feel an evil inner sense of satisfaction when a person who was regarded as a finer Christian than we turns out to have feet of clay. The same thing happens when the secretary down the hall with a better paying job receives a tongue-lashing from her boss for shoddy work.

Of course, we can define what we are talking about and still deceive ourselves so that we don't recognize jealousy. Especially our own. And when we are self- deceived, we cannot grow.

We are sometimes jealous of brothers and sisters because they seem to get more attention from our parents. We are jealous because they are better looking, or smarter, or have possessions or privileges we don't. Sometimes these jealousies stay with us for a lifetime, destroying us on the inside.

We are sometimes jealous of our husband or wife. Some wives are green with envy because their husbands have more freedom outside the home and more ego fulfillment in life. Some husbands are jealous of their wives' friendships.

We are sometimes jealous of other people at work. Why did he or she get a promotion or honor? I deserved it more. How do they seem to get so much more done with so little apparent effort?

Many jealousies arise because of our involvement with competitive institutions. We are jealous when they surpass us, or achieve greater success. We reveal our jealousy by bad-mouthing them and trying to minimize their accomplishments. This is done in businesses, social institutions, and churches. You've probably heard this: "If we used the gimmicks they use, we'd grow like that, too."

A Case of Jealousies

Sometimes we are jealous of our friends. Years ago in high school a friend and I were considered for membership in the honor society. I was rejected, and I assumed he would be too. But I was shocked to learn he was accepted. I had a terrible case of the jealousies, and it took me a long time to overcome it.

I am also jealous of someone who is a better friend of "X" than I am. Why should they be closer? I want "X" to consider *me* his best friend, not someone else.

We get jealous within the church. Did you ever have problems because you were passed over for elder, or deacon, or Bible class teacher, or song leader, or even communion server? People like me can get jealous because we are passed over as preacher. Some people seethe with jealousy when they see certain people taking a public part in church activity.

And there is romantic jealousy. All of us have probably felt it as teenagers when someone else was going with the person we most wanted to be with. Married couples experience it too. Wives are jealous of the secretary at work. Husbands are jealous if wives spend too much time speaking to other men. Some of these situations are cause for genuine concern. But concern is one thing, and jealousy is another. One of life's greatest hurts is jealousy caused by affairs of the heart.

A Cloud of Jealousy

When a jealous attitude is present, it can break out nearly anywhere. It can center on possessions. It can dwell on abilities or talents. It can be stirred up by adulation or praise given another. Reputation or position can be focal points. The problem is not caused by external circumstances, whatever they are. The problem is in our own hearts.

Jealousy is a terrible thing. Joseph was sold into slavery by his jealous brothers (Acts 7:9). It was the reason the early Christians were persecuted (Acts 5:17; 13:45; 17:5). James says devilish wisdom is characterized by jealousy and selfish ambition. The result, he wrote, is "disorder and every vile practice" (James 3:14-16).

He also says jealousy is one of the causes of war and fighting (4:1, 2). The word for "covet" in verse 2 is the same Greek term translated jealousy. I read in my local paper when a jealous husband, wife, or lover murders his or her spouse. Much of the conflict and hostility in people, though attributed to other causes, is really caused by jealousy.

Have you seen yourself in these last few paragraphs? If you are like me, you have. (It hurts to write it, as well as to read it.) We need help. And sometimes jealousy clouds our reasoning so much that we don't accept help. But let's clear our minds and see what can be done.

Answering Jealousy

First, recognize that everything anyone else has is a gift to them by God. We need to accept what God has done in making others. If they have it because they are Christians and this is how God has helped them grow in Christ, then we certainly don't want to oppose God's gift of grace. How can we criticize God for what he has done?

Second, we need to remind ourselves that we have all we *really* need in Christ. Why should I be jealous of lesser things when I have a greater thing in my relation to God? The writer of Psalms 73 envied wealthy people until he realized that their wealth was nothing compared to the richness of his own fellowship with the Lord (73: 21-26).

Third, as Christians we recall how much has been given for us and to us. We are called to give ourselves for others. The more I give and love, as the Lord did, the more I am free of the mentality which produces jealousy. Generous service is the antidote to jealousy. It is the spirit which is opposite. One drives out the other.

Finally, there is prayer. I'm not going to keep kicking myself for my failures. I know what God wants me to be, and how hard a struggle it is to get there. But I know if I turn it over to him, he will bring me along. So I ask him. And though I grieve over my failures, my chief attitude will be joy over the victories he grants as life continues.

5 THE BRAGGER'S APPETITE

One of the rowdiest scenes of the year occurs each fall in Dallas, Texas, during the state fair just before Texas and Oklahoma play each other in football. Partisans of both schools spend Friday night and early Saturday morning walking up and down Commerce Street, taunting each other, and boasting of their respective teams, institutions, and states. The winning team has "bragging rights" for the year. This scene is probably repeated on a smaller scale in many other places. Whenever people butt heads, bragging seems to be in order.

This problem certainly works its way into the church. Because we know the church in Corinth was broken up into parties (1 Cor. 1-4), we can just imagine the boasting that went on. Part of it dealt with which party had the best preacher, or best teacher. We saw how people prided themselves on the "best" spiritual gifts (1 Cor. 12:21). If you had been a member of the church in Corinth for a few months, you would probably have found all this boasting pretty tiresome. You would have easily understood Paul when he reminded them that love "is not boastful" (1 Cor. 13:4).

This term used by Paul isn't found anywhere else in the New Testament. It means, according to one source, "behaving like a braggart or windbag, boasting or bragging."

Designed to Impress

Many places in the Bible talk about boastfulness. Jesus saw it in the way some people prayed. That's why he warned them against showy prayers designed to impress men. "Go into your closet and pray in secret," he said. "God will see and will reward you" (Matt. 6:5f.). These "public" prayers were boastful because they were an indirect way of bragging about the prayer's piety.

Ananias and Sapphira (Acts 5:1-11) felt like they had to be praised for their generosity when they sold their property and gave their money to the church. Unfortunately, their desire to boast was contradicted by their greed. The result was their lie about the percentage of the sale price they were giving. Their funerals show how deadly a combination pride and greed can be.

The Pharisee in Luke 18:9-14 not only bragged to God about how good he was (as if God didn't already know him), he tried to boost his own ego by putting down another worshiper in the temple. "God, I thank thee that I am not like other men, extortioners, unjust, adulterers, or even like this tax collector. I fast twice a week, I give tithes of all that I get" (Luke 18:11, 12). No wonder he prayed just "to himself." He lacked humility necessary for true prayer.

Boasting is bad enough by itself. But its corruptness is multiplied when it leads to greater wrongs. James pointed this out in his classic statement about the use of the tongue. "So the tongue is a little member and boasts of great things. How great a forest is set ablaze by a small fire" (James 3:5). Bragging, like a fire which can easily get out of control, can do a great deal of damage. Have you ever had a relationship ruined because you couldn't stand someone else's boasting? Or maybe you've been the offender because of your own bragging?

Bragging Rights

Here are some examples of boasting. Have you heard any of these?

"Yes, I know he won. But it was a fluke. He couldn't do it again."

"This year I have preached all over the country. Frankly, I've had more invitations than I can handle."

"You know, I had an experience almost like the one you just described. But in my case the situation was even more unusual and difficult. Let me tell you about what happened to me." (You know how this works. You don't really hear what the other person is saying because you are so busy thinking about your "topper." That way you will get back in the center of the picture.)

"I told them that was the wrong thing to do, but they wouldn't listen. Now they are having real trouble. If they had only listened to me, they wouldn't be in this mess." (Or, "I told you so!" with emphasis on the "I".)

"Oh, that I were judge in the land! Then every man with a suit or cause might come to me, and I would give him justice" (Absalom).

"Let me tell you about the business deal I swung. Man did we generate some big bucks."

"God has given me greater spiritual abilities than you. I even have the gift of tongues. The Holy Spirit works more in my life than in yours."

"Our is the greatest church in this whole area."

"I don't see why he (or she) should have been recognized any more than me. I'm as good and as deserving as him (or her)."

When all else fails, we could even boast, "Well, at least I'm more humble than he is."

The Name-Droppers

There is also the indirect form of boasting, such as name-dropping. You know. "I saw Wilt Chamberlain in the airport the other day." "I was once on the same flight with John Connally." Sometimes I boast by letting people know about the semi-famous person who was once one of my students. When I think about it, I realize no one really cares whom I saw, or rode with, or taught. I am trying to make myself seem more important by associating myself with some well-known person.

So we may boast indirectly by using family, or an organization, or a well-known friend (or acquaintance), or possessions, or the accomplishments of a school or organization. Some people just have to tell you they are members of the country club because it makes them look important. I am sure, too, a lot of money is spent on unnecessary material things just for bragging rights ("Come over and see my new home computer").

Someone may say, "Now just wait a minute. I

don't think all those examples you gave were that bad. After all, it isn't necessarily boasting to tell the truth." Certainly *some* of these statements can be made without bragging. Paul doesn't say we can never say "I." He used that pronoun enough himself! That's true. Just because a person talks about himself doesn't necessarily mean he is bragging.

Protecting Pride

Boasting is wrong when it reflects the wrong kind of self-centeredness. One person may state a truth about himself quite accurately and humbly. The same statement from another person may be bragging. The difference depends on the attitude and intention of the speaker. The first person has no interest in promoting self. The second person is interested in self so much that others are forgotten, and it is hard to love others when you think about yourself too much.

Why do we boast? If we know why, we can make some progress in overcoming it, and it will help give us greater sympathy toward other boasters.

We brag to protect our wounded pride and compensate for failure. When we fail we often assume that proves we are incompetent. To cover that hurt we put up a bluff to pretend we are just the opposite—highly competent. We brag about how good we are to cover up how bad we *think* we are. We do this to remove the sting of defeat, or the pain of rejection in love, or the disgrace of a poor grade on an exam, or the humiliation caused by being "chewed out" at work. Others treat us in a way that makes us seem unimportant. So we talk as if we are extra-important. Sometimes we think the more we brag, the greater our healing will be.

Unfortunately, it often only makes the problem worse. People tend to ignore or "put down" a braggart, so that his sense of rejection is enhanced.

Covering Failure

Besides bragging to cover a temporary defeat, we also brag to cover lasting failures and inadequacies. I know one man who has spent his whole life trying to impress people with his macho image because he has always doubted his masculinity. We see another form of this problem in the Pharasaic attitude condemned by Jesus. The Pharisees paraded their piety to impress others, but Jesus knew that beneath the surface they were people of quite a different sort (Matt. 6:1-18). There are people today who boast of their religion because it is to their advantage to project such an image. But they are actually irreligious. This sort of boasting is hypocritical because it tries to impress others with what is really a false front, worn to cover a failure or flaw. It's better to acknowledge the problem and deal with it through the help of trusted Christian friends.

A third reason to boast is to conceal fear. A boy whistles as he passes the cemetery. If he didn't, he might run with fright. People don't want to show their fears so they choose their very points of greatest anxiety to make the boldest assertions of superiority. The lives of some people become one continuous boast because they are so afraid of life, or of other people, or of the future.

Disguising Insecurity

Another reason people boast is to cover personal insecurity. Some of us with deep inferiority complexes try to cover them up by showing off. The need some people have to be the center of attention may be due to insecurity. This kind of behavior can be a cry for help. I once spent several days with a person who would turn every conversation, after two or three sentences, to himself. What he did became humorous. The rest of us began to talk about it among ourselves. "Is this guy for real?" At first, I was irritated because he wouldn't let us talk about anything but him. But it became obvious that he was a little man tortured by feelings of personal inferiority. He was putting on an act to cover up. His real message was a pitiful "Help! Please notice me!" Tragically, his bragging drove people away and made his feelings of insignificance even worse.

Failures, fears and insecurities are not so much sins as they are problems. The important thing is the way we choose to handle them. All of them contain the seed of a virtue. Feelings of personal inadequacy do let us know we need help. That knowledge may eventually lead us out of ourselves into the healing the Lord offers.

But there is a fifth reason for boasting which is a sin, not just a problem. Some boasters believe they are better than others. Rather than keeping their feelings secret, they blow their trumpets to announce how good they are. It is one thing to know you have superiority in some way, but it is another to attempt to convince others of it.

Focusing on "Me"

Remember that our subject is love, which Paul said is not boastful. Boasting, in the wrong sense, is based on preoccupation with self. It may be a black, diabolical conviction: "I'm better than others, and they need to know it." Or it may be failure, repeated failings, fear, or insecurity. But they all represent a person whose thoughts are centered on self.

A Christian, however, thinks first of God and then of others. Self-centeredness draws in, and is grasping. Christian love reaches out, and is giving. The boaster thinks first of "me." The Christian thinks first of God, then of "you" or "them." Love notices others for their good. Boastfulness wants others to notice self for the benefit of self. C. S. Lewis says pride is essentially competitive. Proud people want to augment self at the expense of others.

Boaster's Need Love Too

Another side of the problem of boastfulness is the effect it has on others. Most people are bored by a boaster. But bragging also belittles others. The other side of "big me" is "little you." If you brag to me, it implies I lack your talent, or status, or possessions (or whatever). That isn't a very loving way to treat others. And we must remember that often a boaster stretches the truth. I want so much to seem important I will even lie.

We need to avoid boasting, but we also need to show compassion to people who are caught in this trap. It is not really a happy way to live. A braggart, no matter how obnoxious, needs love and concern. Sure, it is easier to ignore or even retaliate. But we ought to pray for a special grace from God to help such people. God's love, given through ourselves, may be just what the boaster needs to "kick the habit."

But someone may ask, "How come the New Testament speaks of boasting in the Lord?" A different Greek term for boasting is used here. Also, this boasting praises what God has done, not what man has done. It is actually an humble kind of boasting. Paul emphasized this in writing to Corinth. "For who sees anything different in you? What have you that you did not receive? If then you received it, why do you boast as if it were not a gift?" (1 Cor. 4:7). "I am not going to boast in other men's labors. 'Let him who boasts, boast in the Lord.' For it is not the man who commends himself that is accepted, but the man whom the Lord commends" (2 Cor. 10:17). Paul also said to the Romans, "Then what becomes of our boasting? It is excluded. On what principle? On the principle of works? No, but on the principle of faith" (Rom. 3:27).

The Bragger's Appetite

We don't deny that God has given us a basic appetite for recognition. But the boasting Paul condemns (1 Cor. 13:4) represents a perversion of the proper fulfillment of this hunger. This need is satisfied when we recognize that God knows us and cares about us. He cares about us more than any person or persons. He cares about us even more than we care about ourselves. No matter how much we brag, no human recognition will ever compare with the infinite recognition God has given us through Christ. We don't need to elevate ourselves before men. He has made us competent. Christ sets us free from the burden of boasting by showing us how truly important we are to the Creator and Ruler of the entire universe.

The man whose self-esteem is grounded in the goodness of God has no reason to boast. He understands that his personal worth is not based on high octane performance or stunning appearance, but on the value God attaches to his life through Christ. The Jews lost all cause for nationalistic boasting when they realized that Christ died for the Gentiles too. Love is not boastful because it comprehends God's grace as it works to transform you into a person of worth.

6 THE ARROGANCE EFFECT

I have spent much of my life studying and teaching the Bible. This has involved years of study, both for academic degrees and personal growth. I like to think that I have learned something from all this reading and thinking. In fact, I have been known to flatter myself that I know more than most people. But as sure as I do I am confronted by a younger Christian who thinks he is right and I am wrong on some biblical question. I sometimes think, "Who do you think you are? You have only been learning for a short time, and your understanding is really superficial. I've spent all these years in study and have a Ph.D. I've forgotten things you haven't learned yet. How dare you challenge me?"

I believe I understand what arrogance is. How could I have such an inflated opinion of my own importance? Even if my learning far exceeds that of the other person, I have no right to such an attitude. I get that way when my whole mind centers on *my* dignity, and I act as if what I have were *my* achievement, rather than God's gift.

I don't know what your story is, but I expect if you look closely at your life you can find some problem like the one I've confessed.

The Cream Puff

I don't know how creampuffs are made, but it looks like someone took a biscuit, put some goo on top, pumped some air into the middle, and squirted some more goo into the hole. People can be creampuffs, too. That's a person who is swollen up because he is pumped full of his own importance. He certainly couldn't care very much about me or about anyone else. How could he? He is too full of himself.

A puffed up personality reminds me of a Greek verb related to the word for a bellows. The verb indicates a person who has been inflated or caused to swell, as if by a bellows. Paul uses that verb to describe a particular unloving type of person. It is translated "puffed up," "giving himself airs," "cherishing an inflated idea of his importance," and "being conceited" (1 Cor. 13:5). The RSV translation says, "Love is not arrogant!"

The Arrogance Effect

The idea of someone being pumped up like a balloon suggests a comic figure who would go "whoosh" if punctured. But in a real life situation it's not funny. Paul saw several things that arrogance had done to the brothers and sisters in the church at Corinth.

First, the church had split. Competing religious leaders or teachers, each of whom was the center of a circle of disciples, probably caused the split. The various camps quarreled (1 Cor. 1:11, 12). Each group was impressed with the wisdom and viewpoint of its leader. Perhaps they were also impressed with his manner of teaching. And there may have been competition because of the relative evangelistic successes of each leader and group. Certainly there is nothing wrong with admiring intelligence, preaching skill, leadership ability, or evangelistic expertise. But the competition between the Corinthian groups got so hot and personal that each party was pumping itself up to put the others down. Rather than mutual joy in everyone's abilities, there was a fierce sense of "how good we are" and "how sorry you are."

Paul saw how terrible this pride was. It was exactly opposite to the loving spirit of Jesus. After all, whatever gifts any leader has come from God. There was no room for men to boast. To illustrate the problem, Paul observed that the parties in Corinth were following himself, Cephas, Apollos, and even Christ (in a sectarian sense). He appealed to them to give up their arrogant attitudes. *"I have applied all this to myself and Apollos for your benefit, brethren, that you may learn by us to live according to scripture, that none of you be puffed up in favor of one against another"* (1 Cor. 4:6).

After he wrote, Paul planned to visit the church. He knew the problem might still be unresolved when he got there. As he thought about the confrontation that would result, he wrote, *"Some are arrogant, as though I were not coming to you. But I will come to you soon, if the Lord wills, and I will find out not the talk of those arrogant people but their power"* (1 Cor. 4:18, 19). He expected to deal with people who considered themselves above any correction or rebuke. They had a proud spirit, but it would be no match for the "rod" of apostolic power (1 Cor. 4:21).

Moral Arrogance

Second, there was a man in the church at Corinth who was living with his father's wife—apparently his step-mother. Even pagan society avoided this type of incest. Its presence in the Corinthian membership had even brought the church below worldly standards. It was bad enough for the sin to occur, but to Paul's shock the church showed no moral outrage. They allowed the situation to exist without any sign of grief. They were arrogant. We can only guess why. Perhaps they had become morally insensitive. Perhaps the division had made each party so defensive it would not admit sin among its number. Perhaps they felt they were above the "rules" by which others were bound. But the sinners needed loving rebuke so that their lives might be restored to God's favor. Paul insisted that this insolent arrogance be crushed. He called for immediate discipline of the offender (1 Cor. 5:1-5).

And third, there was a problem with "knowledge" possessed by people who considered themselves mature Christians (1 Cor. 8:1). I have had students who felt they had such an advanced view of Christianity they were above the do's and don'ts which applied to lesser mortals. They had escaped legalism into a more spiritual view. They felt they were close to God in spirit even if they ignored his commandments. The people in Corinth may have been the same way. The issue there was eating meat left over from sacrifice to an idol. It was good meat, and Christian people had the right to eat it. As far as they were concerned, idols were nothing. It was simply steak or roast, nothing more. But some of the "weaker" Christians hadn't thought the matter through, and to them eating this meat was a genuine wrong.

So Paul called upon the mature brethren to consider the weaker. "Now concerning food offered to idols: we know that 'all of us possess knowledge.' 'Knowledge' puffs up, but love builds up" (1 Cor. 8:1). Christians shouldn't assume "superiority" just because they may have a better understanding of a matter. Christianity calls for humility and service, not arrogance and unconcern. No one in Christ should be puffed up over another. Lowliness is the key to discipleship. In fact, the higher one gets, the lower he has to descend. The Highest of all became the lowest of all.

Super Christians

We learn from these three cases that arrogance had infected the Corinthian church like a disease. It was an attitude which only awaited an occasion. I'm sure it was also at work in the lawsuits between brethren, the abuses of worship, and the misconceptions in doctrine. These problems should have been solved. But at Corinth, people were so sold on themselves that no answers could come until some haughty spirits were broken. To do that, Paul confronted them with the power of God's word. No one was so important, or knew so much, or was so mature that he was exempt from the need for humility and repentance. To be God's person is to be honest with yourself, admit fault, and swallow pride.

These three cases use the same terminology which is translated "arrogant" in 1 Cor. 13:5. The term is also used in Col. 2:18 to describe the people who accepted a heretical view combining elements of Judaism, angel worship, and extreme asceticism. These heretics saw themselves as super Christians. They implied others were not spiritual, committed, or close to God unless they accepted the same view. They may have boasted, "Join us, and become a *real* Christian!" Paul says they were "puffed up without reason" by a "sensuous mind." Besides being seriously wrong in denying the full power of Christ to save men, they had a horrible attitude.

Intellectual Pride

Arrogance is a person's overwhelming sense of his own importance. For example, a person may be blessed with superior intelligence. There is nothing wrong with knowing you are bright, if you are. But an arrogant person knows it, is proud of it, lets others know it, makes them uncomfortable with it, and generally thinks he is above people with lesser intelligence. Consider the same gift coupled with a loving spirit which uses intelligence as God's gift to enrich others by teaching, counseling, or encouraging.

People can become arrogant because of their education. The Gnostics of biblical times believed they had an inside knowledge which unspiritual people did not possess. Thus they considered themselves superior. If you live around a university, as I do, you know that knowledge and arrogance are often found together. I know a brilliant teacher who constantly uses his superior learning to intimidate and degrade his students. Because of it they resent him. Also, a student once told me of the arrogance displayed by the students of a certain university because of the reputation of their school. They come in a room with an attitude which says, "Knowledge has arrived."

I have noticed, too, when educated people in the church speak patronizingly of the ignorance of other believers. Sometimes Christian "intellectuals" betray this attitude by a nod or sly smile to one another while in the presence of those of lower attainments. They seem to say, "Look at this ignoramus. How could he believe anything as stupid as that?" If you believe your learning has made you better than someone else, beware. It is a symptom of spiritual sickness.

It can work the other way also. People assume superiority because of lack of formal education. This spirit delights in slighting or ridiculing academic degrees, institutions of learning, or leading thinkers. If you scorn others because they are "eggheads," you too need to be alarmed over your spiritual condition.

In both cases, the real point of Christianity is forgotten. Knowledge or lack of it is not to be valued as an end in itself. The important thing is our service to Christ. We can't serve others if we "put them down" because they are not like us.

The Superiority Syndrome

What about racial arrogance? Hopefully, we are past the worst of the horrors of civil rights conflicts. But people say there is still enormous prejudice in this country. The Klan is still marching, and that stirs racial insults and riots. People assume they are automatically superior to others because of their pigmentation. Arrogance breaks out in the use of names like "honky" and "nigger."

Jesus has destroyed such barriers and made all Christians one in himself. This did away with any taint of racial superiority in a Christian's thoughts and speech. The servant follower of a servant Christ should have no room in his heart to consider himself superior. In fact, he makes himself the servant of people of a different race. We need to avoid developing clever ways of concealing racial arrogance, even from ourselves.

Less than 200 yards from my office is the house of one of the most prestigious sororities at the university where I teach. Membership at some of these "upper crust" fraternities and sororities sometimes involves wearing a certain kind of clothing, assuming a certain style of life, and looking down on other students who aren't good enough to be "one of us." This is arrogance of social status or group. It happens many places besides universities. I have seen it in honor societies, civic organizations, military components, business firms, and even in social clubs at Christian colleges. People assume a superiority because they are in the inner ring. They draw an inflated sense of self-worth from the group and look down on others. Christians, however, look up to others from that lowly place where they wash feet.

Some people become haughty because of their material possessions. They flaunt what they have to embarrass those who do not. Arrogance due to wealth may have been the sin of the rich man in Luke 16:19-31. Could a heart centered on wealth have made him feel superior to the starving Lazarus who eventually died outside his door?

Also, cultural arrogance assumes people from your country are superior to those from other countries. This attitude in a missionary can destroy his effectiveness in a foreign land. It can be regional, too. I have heard arrogant references to Yankees, southerners, and Texans.

Arrogant Convictions

I have also known people who were puffed up because they felt they knew the truth and others didn't. Some people get an enormous boost from feeling they are among the few who are "right" religiously. It is certainly important to believe the right thing. But convictions, no matter how strong, must be held humbly. Arrogant people, when they get into religious discussions, are more concerned about defending themselves than trying to understand God's will.

It figures that an arrogant person can't really discuss. Discussion involves give and take, and indicates some change may be necessary. But arrogant people are not open to change. In fact, they often get so emotional they completely forget about reason. There is no sense in weighing the evidence since their minds are already made up. Deliver me from a "discussion" with such a person.

An arrogant spirit does not really depend on a person's superiority. It is caused by self-centeredness—by not caring about others and looking down on them. Christians know that any superiority we might have is a gift from God. It is given by him so we can use it to serve him and others.

If our hearts are wrong, arrogance can and will crop up anywhere. The only solution is the new outlook toward others we gain when we love people as Jesus loved them.

What can we do about arrogance? We must recognize it, then we must ask God to create within us a new heart so that we will truly regard others with the same serving spirit that is found so beautifully in Jesus. He will help us, but he cannot force his way into our lives. We must ask him.

7 ⁝ᴴᴱ RUDENESS BARRIER

Our search for a definition to "love is not rude" is a bit complicated. Most of the occurrences of these words deal with sexual matters. It isn't quite as easy as it was in studying jealousy, patience or arrogance to break through to what Paul is saying.

In 1 Corinthians 13:5 Paul uses the word *aschēmoneō*. The verb has two meanings. One is "behave disgracefully, dishonorably, indecently," and the other is "to feel that one ought to be ashamed." The first indicates what you do, and the second indicates how you feel.

Besides 1 Corinthians 13:5, the only other passage with the first meaning is 1 Corinthians 7:36-38. This passage is one of the real puzzlers in the New Testament. There are two different ways to translate it, and both are correct in terms of the Greek. You can get the idea by comparing the text and its footnote in your Bible. One way of translating these verses concerns a father and his virgin daughter. "If a father thinks that he is *acting unfairly*" toward his daughter by not allowing her to marry, then he should permit her to wed. This translation ("acting unfairly" are the key words) indicates it is "disgraceful, dishonorable" to forbid her marriage "if she is past the bloom of her youth."

The other translation assumes that the text refers to a man and his fiance. Here is a man "not *behaving properly* toward his betrothed." He should go ahead and marry her "if his passions are strong." This interpretation implies the possibility of sexual impropriety between the two.

Whether it is a father "acting unfairly" toward his daughter, or a man "behaving improperly" toward his beloved, both fit the first basic definition of the verb given above.

Nothing Shameful

The second definition, "to feel that one ought to be ashamed," is used in the Greek Old Testament in Deuteronomy 25:3. A man judged guilty was to be beaten in proportion to his offense. But the stripes were not to exceed forty, since exceeding this limit would cause him to "be degraded in your sight." "Degraded" implies the shame he would feel when the punishment went too far.

The second definition is also found in Ezekiel 16:7. Israel is described as a woman at various stages of life. When she reached full maidenhood, she is described as being naked (our term). Her nakedness was shameful, since in verse eight God covers it and enters into covenant with her.

The noun form of this word also has two definitions. One refers to a shameful deed, as in Romans 1:17 where it indicates homosexuality. The other definition is "shame," relating to the genitalia. This implies nudity. Exodus 20:26 uses it to refer to the "nakedness" of the priest. The expression "anything indecent" in Deuteronomy 23:14 seems to refer to nakedness. And in Revelation 16:15 the term is translated "naked."

The basic definition of the adjective is "shameful, unpresentable, indecent." One pagan writer applies this meaning to sexual activity. In Genesis 34:7 the term describes the sexual defilement of Dinah by Shechem. Deuteronomy 24:1 speaks of a man who marries, then later divorces because he finds "some indecency" in his wife. The exact meaning has been heavily debated, but it is clear that something shameful is indicated. Finally, in 1 Corinthians 12:23 the adjective is translated "unpresentable," referring to the private parts.

The common idea is shame. When Paul says, "Love is not rude," he must mean love does nothing shameful or disgraceful. If I do something to shame or disgrace myself (a lack of healthy self-love), it is unfortunate and has little to do with love. Love involves me and someone else. Therefore in 1 Corinthians 13:5 the definition must be understood as it applies to relationships. Love must not cause offense or shame to another person. It will not humiliate, belittle, or be inconsiderate since all these things shame our fellow man. But surely Paul has more in mind than just sexual matters. Flagrant misuse of sexuality is a shame, and so are other inconsiderate and boorish acts which demean others.

We don't overcome rudeness by keeping rules. We do it by becoming considerate and caring, like our Lord. We are all inconsiderate in some areas of life.

Common Courtesy

You may think my first application of Paul's words isn't very important. But it may be the first that comes to mind when we read "love is not rude." I am thinking of good manners, or courtesy. Our parents taught many of us courtesy from early childhood. It included things like saying "thank you," holding open a door, not crowding into line, offering a chair, and treating our elders with respect. These things sometimes seemed too formal to me, and even occasionally seemed silly. But I was being taught to consider the rights and feelings of others. I was taught not to put myself first.

I remember older folks would mention Emily Post or Amy Vanderbilt in discussions about good manners. When I finally read the introduction to Amy Vanderbilt's book on etiquette, I was impressed by how much sense it made. She said all the mysteries of etiquette were really ways of being thoughtful toward others. That probably is what Paul meant by "love is not rude."

"Those are such small things that you are mentioning," you might say. "Surely they are not important enough to include in a book on love." But Jesus said if a person is not faithful in a little he will not be faithful in much (Luke 16:10). He was speaking of money, but we can adapt the principle. If I don't care about others—their needs, emotions, reactions and sense of self-worth—then my attitude will show in both small and big things. A selfish man is selfish with a small amount and a large amount. The way I act in small things reflects my basic attitude to others. That is a big thing. It is what I am, and it will control every part of my life.

Thoughtless Behavior

Are we rude when we drive our cars? Do we do thoughtless and inconsiderate things like opening our car door in a parking lot and bumping the side of the next car, scraping off some paint? How thoughtful are we if we pollute the environment? How rude are we if we dump our litter on the side of the road? Is it considerate to waste energy? Isn't it rude to be inattentive, or even disrespectful, to a public speaker? Or how considerate is it to dial into the middle of someone else's phone conversation without first listening to see if the line is in use? In conversation, do we thoughtlessly interrupt another speaker? Isn't the individual who continually nags violating this aspect of love? Isn't it rude to disturb others while they are worshipping God (passing notes, nudging, giggling)?

You can probably think of many additions to that list. But look out, though, because it is easy to get away from rude and unloving matters into pet peeves. In fact, you may think I have included a few of my own. But I hope you get the point. If so, you can be more sensitive in the future—not in order to find fault in others, but to root out your own rude attitudes and actions.

Cultural Rudeness

Rudeness also relates to the customs and standards of a society. Each society has its moral standards and its characteristic cultural practices. Of course, a violation of morals is wrong, but let me talk about cultural practices. Those who have traveled out of the United States may have been embarrassed because they did something that was simply not done in the country visited.

Missionaries continually confront this matter of cultural "rudeness." I understand that in Brazil it is considered obscene to make the "OK" sign generally accepted in the United States. In Thailand it is extremely rude, when sitting, to allow the soles of the feet to be pointed at another person. In Australia it is very bad taste (even profane) to use certain words which are commonly used in this country.

Then there is the Argentine student who was in one of my classes. One Saturday he and his wife were driving around campus. Football season was in full swing, and he saw students making the hand sign used by supporters of the university. The student was bewildered. The same sign in his country, he later explained, means "your wife is with another man," and he thought everyone was making it at him.

Many who travel are going to goof simply from ignorance. But if we knew better and still did it, that would be rude and unloving. And without love we are nothing.

Considering Others

In this country, we have similar problems. For example, some styles of dress might be rude and inconsiderate to some people but not others. Methods of dress intended to excite lust in others would certainly not be in order for Christians. Language which would be offensive to others would be rude. It may be unloving to discuss certain topics in certain places. I can't give all the illustrations, and I am not trying to make a set of rules. The key is a geniune interest in and consideration for others.

The same principle works in the church. Suppose I am working with a congregation where all the members read from a translation of the Bible which I dislike. If I were to force my preference upon them (even presuming I could), it would be rude and thoughtless. They may have spent years with their translation and learned to love it. I certainly could present my case, but I must consider their feelings. After all, I don't want them forcing me to use their translation, so why should I try to force them to use mine?

Or consider a church where young people have more "progressive" ideas and older people are more traditional. They are bound to disagree on a number of things. The important thing they must remember is that "love is not rude." The young people must appreciate tradition and those who hold to it, and older people must appreciate progress and those who advocate it. And each group ought to behave so that it is easier for people who disagree with them to love them.

The Rudeness Barrier

There are several scriptures which illustrate what we have been discussing. The first two come from 1 Corinthians 8 and 10. Paul argues that "food offered to idols" can be eaten without sin since idols have no real existence (1 Cor. 8:4-7). But not all people know this. Food is morally neutral, but some people, by eating such meat, might damage their faith. The Christian who insisted on his own rights to eat, at the expense of another's relation to the Lord, would defeat the purpose of the cross. So Paul vowed to avoid eating meat if it caused a brother to fall. Rudeness is the antithesis of the gospel, the former builds barricades while the latter destroys them. Any act that blocks a brother's growth is rude.

In 1 Corinthians 10 the principle is similar, but the specific situation relates to eating food sold in the meat market. Such food could be eaten without questions of conscience. But if someone wished to abstain because the meat came from a pagan sacrifice, Paul called on his brethren to respect that person's decision. He was concerned most about leading others to salvation so he encouraged Christians to "give no offense to Jews or to Greeks or to the church of God, just as I try to please all men in everything I do, not seeking my own advantage, but that of many, that they may be saved" (10:31f.).

Paul talks about similar concerns in Romans 14, except that diet and the observance of holy days are the issues. His concern was that nothing should be done that would injure a brother (14:15), that all things would be for peace and mutual upbuilding (14:19), and that nothing be done which would make someone fall or stumble (14:20f.).

Rumors of Rudeness

A good example of concern for others from Paul's life is given in Acts 21. When he returned to Jerusalem from his third tour, the elders told him about certain rumors that had been spread about him. The Jewish Christians had been "told about you that you teach all the Jews who are among the Gentiles to forsake Moses, telling them not to circumcise their children or observe the customs" (21:21). To dispel these reports they urged Paul to go to the temple with some men who were undergoing purification and to pay for their expenses.

These charges against Paul were false, and he

might have become angry and refused the concession asked of him. Why should he waste his time submitting to the opinions of those who would not go to the trouble to find out or tell the truth about him? But Paul practiced love, which is not rude. He was sensitive to the situation, and he wanted to do the greatest good for his brothers. He went with the men, and consequently he almost lost his life. But the point is his sensitivity. He was sacrificing no moral point, and he was doing what he could to promote unity within the church.

The Sexually Rude

Remember our definitions say love does not "behave disgracefully, dishonorably, indecently." Aside from 1 Corinthians 13:5, which is a general statement, we noted ten passages, all of which indicate sexual concerns implied by the term.

We live in a culture where public nudity is becoming common. A sexual revolution is ocurring. There is decreasing moral opposition to illicit sexual activity. Our society needs to be reminded of the biblical perspective. In the Old Testament nakedness was considered a shame. The New Testament tells Christians to abstain from sexual relations outside marriage. It stresses fidelity to one's own mate. Violation of these is considered shameful, and is to be avoided by the disciple of Jesus.

But we are talking about sexual "rudeness" as a lack of consideration for others. Isn't it true that modern sexual attitudes often deny the value of the whole person? They focus only on a physical, even a genital, relation. Women are often considered as merely sex objects. People discuss and practice sexual relationships in ways that ignore deeper spiritual, emotional, and psychological needs for genuine love. People think their need for love can be satisfied simply by physical sexual relations using the proper techniques. But this only intensifies the need for genuine person-to-person interaction.

This emphasis on the physical dehumanizes us. It brings us to the level of the beast of the field. People are used as a means to physical gratification. Then they are put aside for other involvements. It indicates to others that they are only useful to us for the temporary pleasures their bodies can afford. This insults the emotional, intellectual, and spiritual dimensions of a person. People seem to say, "I have no concern at all for the real person you are. You are, to me, only an apparatus I use for immediate sensual pleasure." To me, this is the ultimate rudeness or insensitivity.

This is not meant to be a long list of rules for avoiding rudeness. But let us be sensitive to others and consider their thoughts and feelings. Let us not deliberately shame them by our behavior. This is love, and without love we are nothing. It is not always easy to maintain this, but God will help us. His strength is made greater in our weakness. Carry your shortcomings to him. Your attitudes and your whole life can be changed by his power.

8 THE INSISTING SELF

When I was a kid I collected games. I had almost 150, and my room became the neighborhood recreational center. One of our favorite games was Monopoly. Each of us had a favorite marker. My favorite was the orange one. But some of the others also liked the orange piece best. One day a friend named Don, who also liked the orange marker, came over to play. We both wanted the same piece. I wasn't about to give in, and neither was he. I had the advantage, though, since I owned the game. We sparred stubbornly for a while, and neither gave in. Finally Don left and went home, and neither of us got to enjoy playing. But my pride was intact. I insisted on my own way to the very end.

Now I am not proud of how I acted. I was stubborn and selfish, like the guy who threatens to take his ball and go home if the game isn't played his way. Of course, those were kid's games, and they usually just make us smile. But it is not funny to realize that many adults still have not progressed beyond this juvenile attitude. As a matter of fact, selfishness is really the besetting sin of all humanity. If we could solve this spiritual problem, society would be miraculously improved.

Paul's statement in 1 Corinthians 13 that "love does not insist on its own way" stands almost in the middle of his list of the characteristics of love. It's in the middle another way, too. Every quality we have examined, positive or negative, relates to whether we first seek our own way, or first seek to serve God and others. "Love does not insist on its own way" could be a heading with the others being subheadings explaining various parts of it.

Self-Interest

I often find a misunderstanding of selfishness that burdens people with unnecessary guilt. They feel anytime they think about themselves or do something for themselves they are being selfish. Not so. After all, you are inside your own skin and think with your own brain. You naturally care about your own welfare. You need to eat, stay comfortable, be fulfilled, and feel useful. And you certainly want to enjoy present and final union with God. There is nothing wrong with that. Otherwise, God wouldn't have made us the way he did if there was.

There is a difference between selfishness, which is wrong, and self-interest, which is healthy. But we must put the two in the right relationship. Self-interest is the legitimate consequence of the way God has created us. Selfishness is the mark of fallen man. It is the desire to make self the center of the universe, to put self before all else.

Self-interest says I need sleep. But a friend is having a marriage crisis. Because I am concerned, I give up most of a night's sleep to help him. I may even give up sleep for several nights. To refuse to help him so I can get my sleep would be selfish. However, the time may come when I have lost so much sleep I must rest or collapse. In that case, if I force myself to stay awake it will do neither him nor me any good. So I get my sleep. Then I can come back rested, better able to help him.

Consider Jesus. His self-interest led him to pray in the garden for the cup to be taken away. The impending suffering was as horrible for him as it would have been for us. But when it became clear he could do God's will only by drinking it, he would have been selfish to refuse. He gave up his self-interest for the greater good—the cross and the salvation of mankind.

Disciplined Thinking

God made us to be servants. To do that, we need health, energy, rest and food. We do what we must to have these things, not just for our own sake, but because they help us serve others. Recreation is important because it re-makes us. Re-made, we return to give ourselves away. But if we insist on our recreation at any cost, that's selfish. I jog daily because it improves my physical condition and energy level. But sometimes people need me at my jogging time. If I jogged and did not counsel them, that would be selfish. But if I omit exercise completely, I may be less effective because I'm less healthy.

Every bit of interest I have in myself, then, has

to be considered in terms of my relation to God or others. If I retreat from serving God and others and do only what pleases me, I move into the prison cell of my own ego. And there is nothing in the universe smaller than a person who is locked up inside "me."

To avoid insisting on our own way, we must discipline our thinking. We must analyze the way we think. How much of our thinking centers on God? How much on concern for others? How much on self? Do we think of the needs, happiness and feelings of others? Never? Some? Often? Always? What do we customarily make first priority? Self? Others? How do we view time, energy, property, and money? In terms of self? Or others? Do we consider others as important as self? Do their rights rank as high as ours in our minds? Are we always biased in favor of ourselves? Would we admit we were wrong to accept pain or give up a "right" on behalf of someone else? Just how do we think?

The Mind of Christ

First, we must have the "mind of Christ." Though his eternal nature and glory is beyond our imagination, he descended to the lowliest of earth's situations and died the death of a disgraced criminal because of God's love for man. Note the powerful description of his self-emptying in Philippians 2:5-11. He came to serve and give his life a ransom for many (Matt. 20:28). He humbly washed his disciples' feet (John 13:12-17). He became poor so that we might become rich (2 Cor. 8:9). He loved us and gave himself up for us, a fragrant offering and sacrifice to God (Eph. 5:1f.).

The cross should motivate us. We are called to

self-denial, as he denied himself. It was Jesus, who gave all, who called the rich man to sell all and give to the poor (Matt. 19:16-30). To follow Jesus is to daily take up the cross (Luke 9:23). Life can be saved only by losing it (Mark 8:25). Even those close to us by emotional ties must rank behind our discipleship to Jesus (Luke 14:25-26). We must renounce all we have to be his disciples (Luke 14:33).

Paul repeats this call to service in other places. Those of us who are Christ's offer our bodies as living sacrifices (Rom. 12:1). We die with Christ (Rom. 6:3f.). Our old self is renounced (Rom. 6:6-11; Gal. 2:20). Many other passages bear witness to the giving and serving genius of Christianity. So when we forget that "love does not insist on its own way," our entire Christian profession goes awry.

The Lord said it very simply: "Do unto others as you would have them do unto you." We must put ourselves where others are and ask what we would want done to us if we were them. We must keep in mind that the greatest good for any one is doing God's will. We must consider how others will be affected by a word, action, policy, or even by silence. That doesn't mean all decisions will be easy. Some cases are complex. But if we follow the golden rule, we come at problems from the right direction. We do the best we can, and pray for God to guide us.

The Mind of Man

What is our motivation for acquiring money or material things? What do we want? How do we want to use a higher salary, an expensive car, a work of art, a boat, or a fine home? How much human suffering have we caused by selfishness about material things? How much crime is caused by greed? How much are our economic crises caused by selfishness on the part of labor, management, or government? How many people have compromised their values because of avarice? Considering what we have said about selfishness, what do you think of the philosophy which says a product or service should be sold for the highest price the market can bear?

We are often selfish because of our special interests (even in the church). This keeps us from being fair to other interests, and often leads to competition between churches in the same town. It happens when people are more concerned about promoting the interests of their congregation than they are about working to God's glory. It can result in criticism of other congregations. A prospective member might slip away from "us" to "them."

Our culture stresses the importance of climbing the ladder, whether socially or in business, politics, and education. But this tempts people to become selfishly centered on their own importance and their progress. The "climber" sometimes hurts others in the process. How can a person who is determined to "get ahead" at any cost relate to love that does not insist on its own way?

Around us we see competition in business, athletics, personal relations, academics—nearly everywhere. Much of the culture of this country is built on competition. In its right place, competition can be a healthy thing. But it is sometimes prostituted by being coupled with selfishness. When that happens, people who try to get a competitive edge can't afford to think of others. Fierce competition usually does one thing to others, while love does the opposite.

Motives for Service

Another way to apply the unselfishness of love is to consider our vocations. Of course, nothing is wrong with making a living. We have the right to be paid for goods or services which we supply others. However, it is important to examine our motives because we can easily go beyond what is right and proper. Are we interested in our jobs because they are avenues of service? Do we consider them as ministries, even as worship to God (Rom. 12:1f.)? Paul cautioned Christians not to steal, but to work honestly with their hands so they would "be able to give to those in need" (Eph. 4:28).

If you are a Christian automobile mechanic, are you primarily interested in helping others, or are you interested in separating your customers from as much of their money as possible? If you are a Christian doctor, is your priority healing the sick, or is it the amount of income you can generate? Are you so consecrated to helping that you would do it for nothing if necessary? And if you had a rich patient who would pay a great deal, would you charge as much as possible to enrich yourself, or would your rate be in line with what you charge a poor patient?

How does the call to avoid insisting on one's own way apply to professional athletes, insurance salesmen, real estate brokers, military officers, secretaries? How about Christian book sellers? What if you are a builder, or an assembly line worker, or a cab driver? Suppose you are spending a summer selling religious books and Bibles. Would you sell a customer a book he didn't need and would never use just to make money? Or would you tell a customer not to overspend if you felt he needed the money more for something else? If you are a student, are you learning so you can serve your fellow man, or just for what you can get out of it? Are there some jobs a Christian should not take because they demand "insisting on your own way"?

Insistence in the Family

These are hard questions. I don't know how I would answer all of them. I don't know if I would even be honest enough with myself to know the right answers. But I know I must take Christ's call seriously in all parts of my life. It isn't easy to examine my motivations. But I must try to discover *why* I do what I do. Who do I really consider "No. 1" in my life?

We also may find selfishness in our personal relationships. A selfish husband refuses to consider his wife's needs, or sees her only as a person to satisfy his desires. Is she an important part of decisions, or are they dumped on her with a "like it or lump it" attitude? Some husbands misinterpret Paul's words about the husband being the head of the wife. They forget the part about loving her as Christ loves the church, and emphasize the idea of the "authority." They act like tyrants, browbeating their wives into submission with a misapplication of the Bible.

Wives can be guilty, too. They can get petulant and peevish when they don't get their own way. They can nag and nag and nag until the husband, out of sheer frustration, gives them what they want.

Parents are in a position of authority in the home, but they can selfishly ignore the real needs of their children to avoid spending time or money to keep from giving up something for the sake of the kids. Children can be selfish. A tantrum is basically a selfish act. Some children try to manipulate their folks to get their own way.

Employer and employee, teacher and student, captain and private, supervisor and laborer—these and any other relationships offer us the chance to be selfish or to be servants.

The Insisting Self

By our very nature, we tend to be selfish. No matter how thoroughly we examine our lives, we will always miss something. We will fail. But we should not become discouraged. God knows our problems. He will bear with us and give us the resources we need as we struggle. We will make progress by his power. A skirmish lost does not mean total defeat in the war. We hold on to our ideals. When we fall we cry for mercy and strength, and we rise again. Over and over. God does not lose patience with us. He is making us more fit for final fellowship with him. He does not give up on us, and we must not give up on ourselves.

If we do "insist on our own way," we are chasing a mirage. Everything we have has been given us. We have no "own way." If we deceive ourselves by insisting on it, we will be defeated. God runs the universe, and it must operate the way he wills. Can I, a finite human, deny this great and awful truth, and try to make the Lord of all bow to my terms? Of course not! It would be foolishness to think I could. Selfishness is not only contrary to the basic nature of Christianity, but it is everlastingly and infinitely futile!

9 THE IRRITATION EXPLOSION

It usually happens to me about 4:30 or 5:00 in the afternoon. My wife, unfortunately, is usually with me then so she gets the brunt of it. I think I am a reasonable person, ruled by my intellect. But in the afternoon something builds up inside and I sometimes become dangerous. I have been going all day, facing pressures and demands. Finally, hot and hungry, I can't take any more. I want to get mad, or argue, or tell someone off, or just scream.

Sometimes my wife has the same feelings. Fortunately, after 25 years we have learned how to deal with the situation. A good meal preceded by 30 minutes of silence works wonders. But in the early days of our marriage, when one of us exploded it could be grim. To make it worse, when one blew up that generally triggered the other. Then we had some real fireworks!

This comes to mind when I read Paul's statement that "love is not irritable" (1 Cor. 13:5). This statement commands attention from harried mothers, people stuck in traffic jams, workaholic executives, and phone callers put on hold for 30 minutes.

The word *paroxysm* refers to a sudden, violent action or emotion, like my experience each afternoon. It can even mean a convulsion or fit. It is the Anglicized form of the Greek word for the explosion I have been describing. It happens in the mind, and the body often follows. In 1 Corinthians 13:5, Paul tells us not to explode.

What's a Paroxysm?

Three other New Testament passages use this word, and they illustrate that an "explosion" can be either good or bad. Acts 17:16 describes Paul's visit to Athens. Seeing a city full of idols, his spirit was "provoked" within him. This *paroxysm* stirred him to begin preaching daily in the market place. We do not know if he was moved by anger, grief, or a surging impulse to share Christ with pagans doomed to spiritual disappointment. Whatever the case, the circumstances in Athens caused an intense inner experience that moved him to action.

Hebrews 10:24 gives us another pertinent message: "And let us consider how to stir up one another to love and good works . . . " "Stir up" comes from the term we are discussing. The author advises us to help each other to overcome lethargy. "Find ways to jolt each other. Consider what can be done to promote zeal. Promote paroxysms!" That seems to be the idea. Notice that here the explosion is a good and necessary thing.

Another reference, Acts 15:39, describes a "contention" between Paul and Barnabas about the qualifications of John Mark as a missionary. It wasn't an academic discussion about the merits and demerits of a man. There was considerable passion. Two men exploded at each other, and the explosions blew them far enough apart they went their separate ways.

We need to do some further exploring. Obviously not all paroxysms are bad. We need to learn which paroxysms are good and which are not.

Healthy Anger

Anger can be a paroxysm, but Paul says anger isn't necessarily wrong. He said, "Be angry but do not sin" (Eph. 5:26). As a matter of fact, anger in the right place can be a great virtue. Jesus probably experienced it when he cleansed the temple. There his anger powerfully taught the purpose of the holy premises. This case suggests an "anger explosion" is acceptable in certain circumstances. For example, if it leads you to uphold the truth, protect human rights, oppose rampant evil, or defend an important principle.

In 1 Corinthians 13:5, Paul isn't concerned with other kinds of explosions. Since love concerns people, he obviously considers irritation that occurs in human relations. I may become irritated because the alarm doesn't ring, or the plane is late, or the crowd is too large to get to an appointment on time. But if I only explode at a clock or at a delay, I haven't hurt anyone else. It would be different if I threw the clock at my wife, or lost my temper and chewed out the airline ticket agent, or began knocking people over to get through the crowd. Those would be violations of love.

Irritation that comes of ego-centricity harms

95

others and self. Self-centeredness makes us explode at others, and it is the opposite of patience discussed in chapter two. If you think about the times you blew up, inside or outside, you will probably realize you were thinking about yourself. "How dare they waste *my* time by their slowness!" "What right has she to take *my* argument so lightly!"

If I am loving and set my heart on concern for others, then their faults do not exasperate me—their slowness, rudeness, undesirable character traits, inefficiency, or talkativeness. Whether we are irritable with others or not depends on whether we are selfish or selfless. The person filled with concern for others will still likely experience paroxysms, but he will not let them generate hostility to others. They are absorbed by concern for others in which his life is immersed.

I recently sat on the bench at a college football game and watched a well-known coach in action at close range. He certainly had plenty of paroxysms during the game. Some of them he expressed quite openly. But I never saw him berate a player just to satisfy his own ego. He was always concerned about the player's improvement. In fact, that is his philosophy of coaching. He constantly tries to improve them as players and persons. He could easily think about himself first, but he doesn't.

Getting Out-of-Hand

Here are a few examples of how explosions can get out of hand. They are not meant to criticize any particular person. Aren't we all guilty of some of these faults?

A customer was shopping in a department store at the end of a busy day, and a salesperson lashed out at her for no apparent reason.

A young man was playing his guitar in a college dormitory. He was playing too loudly to suit a student in a nearby room, so he asked him to stop or to play softly. The musician, if he had been loving, should have been willing to do so. But he didn't. So the disturbed person came into the room, hit the guitar player, knocked him across the room, and broke his jaw.

A motorist, in frustrating "stop and go" traffic, was accidentally bumped from behind (not very hard) by another car. The first driver jumped out of his car, rushed to the car behind him, reached through the window, grabbed the driver by the neck, and threatened physical violence in quite colorful language.

A traveler stopped his car on a service station parking lot to use an outdoor pay telephone. He was shocked when an angry station attendant chastised him bitterly for having parked on the station premises.

Terrible consequences often follow explosive irritation. It can be a "sin in haste, and repent at leisure," kind of thing. In an unguarded moment, you may say a word or commit an action that may take years to live down. We may open wounds that take a long time to heal, destroy personal relationships, create resentments, generate hard feelings, and start a chain of events that may lead to worse results.

You may be thinking of other examples, perhaps from your own life. In a moment of irritation, a wife or husband blurts out, "I don't love you, and I'm not sure if I ever loved you!" The person makes an emotional statement in the heat of the moment. If they thought about it, they wouldn't say it. They really don't mean it. It was said to defend an ego, and (maybe) hurt a mate. But the words burn like fire in the person's mind. Statements like this are brought up over and over, even if the couple makes up, and the mate who said the words denies really meaning what was said. The words struck the ego of the offended party, and it takes a long time for the wound to heal. In fact, some people won't let it heal, which is another problem.

Triggering Circumstances

Now I want to make some suggestions to help us deal with the temptation to forget love and explode with irritation. The first concerns what I call "triggering circumstances," situations in life that bring us to the breaking point.

The continuing pressure of work plagues us. Day and night we remember the mountain of unfinished tasks hovering over us. We are eaten up by guilt because of uncompleted jobs. Finally, when the load becomes so great it looks like we can never get it done and the pressure to produce increases, we may come to the breaking point.

Perhaps some problems in personal relations disturb us, and we harm innocent parties because of the pressures.

It may be difficult to be loving because of our bad health. If we are in pain or worry about our health, we may become short-tempered. Once I received a letter critical of one of my sermons. The critic didn't hear me preach it, and missed the point of what I said. But I learned that the individual was suffering a terminal illness, and it was really the disease which had written the letter.

Also, financial worries may obsess us. Maybe a

personal problem of a relative or friend pressures us and keeps us tied up in knots from tension. We may disappoint ourselves so much that we become intensely irritable. Even lack of sleep may produce irritation. If we know our weak points, we will know where to make strong defenses. We need to keep tabs on ourselves. If we know when and how problems come, we can prepare to meet them in advance. Let me go back to my opening illustration in this chapter. Now that I know how I get in the afternoon, I can make a special effort to control myself, be pleasant, and (sometimes) keep my big mouth shut!

Concern for Relationships

Second, we should constantly remind ourselves of the call to service with which God challenges all his people. God could justly be "irritated" with us. To face that would be ultimate terror for us. Yet God chose to serve through a cross. The Son of Man came not to be served, but to serve. We remember that, and it shows us the way he wants us to be.

If I consciously try to be concerned about others, I am not going to make them suffer for my problems. Nor will I assume my ego is so important that it must be gratified, no matter who or what is in my way. If I forget about self and concentrate on others, my mental occasions for irritation will be much fewer.

Third, we need to develop a long-range view of life. If I had the power to see all the consequences of what I do, it would certainly change my behavior. I've had students come to me at least ten years after they were in my class and mention some remark I made in class that hurt them. To me it was so trivial I can't even remember it. But to them it wasn't trivial at all. I wish I could go back and "unsay" what I said.

So when I get irritated I should try to consider how what I am tempted to do will look in the future. How will my words or actions affect others? What will those words or actions do to relationships at my work, home, school, or neighborhood? What will be the consequences in a week, month, or year? How much time will I spend in the future regretting or trying to correct a problem that should never have started if I had taken a long-range view?

Fourth, we need to pray. We should never attempt to overcome a problem without praying about it. Which one of us can define the limits of God's power? Many problems and weaknesses which seemed impossible to solve have been solved when exposed, through prayer, to God's touch. We can pray for the spirit that will help us overcome what otherwise might be "triggering circumstances." We can also pray for self-control to combat pressure that comes from what seems to be unbearable force.

Extinguishing Irritation

Finally, we must recognize that despite our best efforts, we will sometimes fail. Rather than give up, we should recognize that none of us have yet achieved perfect love. God is still working on us and helping us become the perfect creatures he wants us to be. We must be willing subjects, even though we have flaws. We must work to understand why we failed. What was the "triggering cause"? Can such circumstances be prevented in the future? More important, we should look within. What personal attribute led to our outburst? We must learn our motivations and present them to God in prayer. On another day, the victory may come more easily.

To close this chapter, consider this from Chrysostom, a great preacher: "As a spark which falls into the sea hurts not the sea, but is itself extinguished, so an evil thing befalling a loving soul will be extinguished without disquietude." God help us have such inner reserves that no circumstance of life can upset them.

10 THE RESENTFUL MEMORY

Have you ever thought how important your memory is? We orient a large part of our lives with the past. We store up the past and use the experience in present-day living. We learn from it, regret it, laugh at it, weep over it, ponder it, and sometimes try to forget it. Think about that last word—"forget"—because there is a certain kind of forgetfulness that is involved in another aspect of love. "Love," Paul says, "is not resentful."

Spend a few minutes thinking about times you have been mistreated in your life. Go back to pre-school, through the elementary grades, junior high, high school, and college up to the present.

Some of us accept this invitation too eagerly. We have much to remember. Some cases we recall in great detail because the memories are burned into our minds. We recall hurt feelings, times when we have been cheated, and when we have been told lies. We have been lied about. We have been misunderstood by people who ought to have known better. We cannot forget the injury done to someone we love. We were beaten out of some good thing by someone else who was much less deserving.

Do you remember these things resentfully? Do you treasure the memory of the hurts, coupling them with a generous measure of self-pity? Do you allow them to influence your present attitudes and behavior? Do you act cooly toward certain people because of past injuries? Do you avoid speaking to someone because you resent them? Does it lead you to choose sides and cause others to do so? Do you refuse to help others because of what they did to you in the past? Do you gossip about some people because of resentment? Have you tried to smear someone's reputation because you remember how they mistreated you?

Vengeance Is Mine

Because of these resentments, do you want vengeance? "I'll get even with him some day. He can't treat me that way!" Revenge can seem appealing. It almost seems abnormal to resist it. While I am writing this, our country faces a crisis. A foreign nation holds fifty American citizens hostage. People cry for retaliation. When others appeal for calm to prevail, those people feel frustrated by what strikes them as appeasement.

Revenge was a main ingredient for many of the old western shows on TV. A villain would beat-up one of the "good guys" at the beginning of the show. Then we waited for justice to be done, knowing that the bullies would "get theirs" in the end. When the hero punched them out, it gave us a vicarious satisfaction of our desire for revenge. We wouldn't do it ourselves (after all, we are Christians), but we enjoyed seeing it done by someone else. This shows how close to the surface resentment lies for us.

It's too easy for us to double up our fist to strike back, or to think of stinging words we could say in retaliation. We like to get even. We enjoy imagining how our tormentors will writhe in pain after we have paid them back. Even Christians enjoy such thoughts, though they may control their outward behavior quite well. Don't you agree?

Getting Even

What would the world be like if we all kept our resentments until we had gotten even for all the wrongs done to us? Who could stand to live in such a culture? Despite our claim to be civilized, we see far too much vengeance around us. What if *everyone* acted this way, and our entire morality was based on retaliation?

Suppose you are with a group of people you see on a regular basis (a class, civic club, church, or group at work). The group is told that at a given signal everyone is to go to anyone else they like and do whatever they want to avenge any wrongs done to them by that person. Toward what person in the group would you first move? What would you do to them when you got there? Or, on the other hand, who would be moving toward you, and what would they do to you when they reached you?

What would it be like to have a whole society like that? Everyone getting even with everyone else. It would be complete chaos and warfare all

105

the time. Who could stand to live in such a place? There would be no security.

But when we are resentful and vengeful, isn't that the kind of world we are advocating? Go ahead and get even, just remember there is a gun pointed at your back, too. Resentment is a terrible thing. If we have overdrawn this picture of society, it still does not diminish the horror of vengeance.

Resentment Defined

Christians should fight against the natural tendency to resent, because something special has happened to us. Jesus has turned our lives around. Thus Paul's reminder that "love is not resentful" relates to our deepest commitment. Without love we are nothing. With resentment we also are nothing. I may *want* to resent, but because of Jesus I drive these thoughts from my mind. I let the words of recrimination die on my lips. I relax my clenched fists. My frown disappears, to be replaced, in time, by a loving smile.

Two Greek words are translated "resentful." One is the word for evil. The other is the verb meaning to take into account (*logidzomai*). The verb, one of Paul's favorite words, is an accountant's term. Love does not enter evil done to it in a ledger to consider later. No matter what wrong is done, it should not be found in the Christian's account book. If we look at the accounting sheet to determine how to treat someone else, there should be no record of the wrong they have done us.

Notice the richness of the Christian's position expressed by Paul in 2 Corinthians 5:19. "God was in Christ reconciling the world unto himself, not counting their trespasses against them." God has plenty of justification for remembering the evil we have done and for treating us the way we deserve to be treated. I would be a fool if I claim to be so good that God is obligated to bless me. So would you. We have all been pretty shoddy much of the time. But God forgets all that! Because of Jesus, he does not hold those wrongs against us. He does not enter them in some heavenly ledger to be used against us on the final day. This is a blessing we don't deserve or fully understand. Think how horrible it would be to face the unleashing of divine resentment against our rebellion.

But God, because of Christ, offers us reconciliation. He rejects the claims of vengeance. He does not want to "get even" with us. He wants to save us. Those who will be saved, he saves. Those who will not, he continues to call and offer salvation.

The Unforgiving Spirit

God has pardoned us. What he has done becomes the basis for our conduct. In Jesus' story of the two debtors (Matt. 18:23-35), a man was forgiven of a debt that today would run into millions of dollars. He promised to "pay all," but there was no way for him to do it. Now how could such a man dare insist that his debtor pay him a few dollars, and even threaten to take his goods and put him in prison if he didn't? The point of Jesus' story is too clear to miss. God has forgiven us so much. We forgiven ones should forgive others. And if we are to forgive, then we must drive resentment out of our lives because it is caused by an unforgiving spirit.

But it is hard not to resent. Our sense of self-importance demands that we get even. Our emotions become involved when we get hurt, so we tend to forget what is reasonable and Christian. We feel no one else has faced a situation quite as difficult as ours. "Certainly others shouldn't resent, but surely God can't expect that of me, knowing all I have had to put up with."

Yet we must try to overcome. God demands it. We must fight the battle, no matter how hard and long it may be.

Keeping Account

Let me discuss a possible misunderstanding before we look at some suggestions.

Paul says love does not keep an account of wrongs. Does that mean all wrongdoing is to be overlooked, to be forgotten? Certainly not. Paul also said civil government must identify wrongdoing and punish the wrongdoer (Rom. 13:1-7). Besides this, Christians must oppose wrong and stand for right. The church should champion the cause of those suffering from oppression (read the book of Amos). We must withstand ungodliness in the community.

Paul says the spirit and practice of personal vengeance are contrary to God's nature. When wrong must be opposed or punished, we should do it with a loving concern for the wrongdoer—with the hope he will repent and turn to his Maker.

I also see a problem here. We can nobly and genuinely claim to be acting "on principle" in opposing wrong. But resentfulness is near and we often fool ourselves. We may be convinced that our motives are good when they are really only a screen to cover a desire for vengeance.

A man once told me of a young lady who was guilty of sexual immorality. He seemed to have a deeply pious concern about her spiritual condition.

I discovered that his real motivation was much less admirable. He had dated her, but she had ended the relationship. He was really coming to me wanting to hurt her by destroying her reputation because she had hurt him. He probably didn't even recognize what he was doing, but I understood what was happening.

When we oppose wrong, and later remember it, we must question our own motives. We may be concealing resentment. Resentment is ungodly, even when concealed beneath a veneer of holiness.

The Revenge Trap

Now for those suggestions promised earlier. First, we need to understand why other persons treat us as they do. Let's apply the golden rule. If we had been in the same circumstances as the other person, how would we have acted? That doesn't excuse what someone else did because their action may have been inexcusable. But why did they do it? Perhaps the offending person faced great pressure or grave disappointment, or came from a dismal background. If I knew what he was going through, it might change how I feel about what he did.

We should be compassionate, not resentful, toward the offending person. That wrong forms a separation from God, and loving people will help the offender find reconciliation. A few years ago the husband of a lovely Christian woman I know was murdered one night at his shop. Police caught the murderer and sent him to prison. She could have spent her years in bitterness (as many have) over the crime. But because of her loving spirit she developed a keen interest in ministering to prisoners where her husband's murderer is jailed. She has shown concern in many ways, including giving money. She wants to help her husband's murderer and others find the Lord.

If we are resentful, we may be as bad as the person who has sinned against us. We certainly can't help people get out of a trap if we are caught in it ourselves. We make things worse, not better, when we add the sin of resentment to the wrong already done. Revenge begets revenge, and both parties become more corrupt.

Second, we need to take a long-range viewpoint—in fact, an eternal viewpoint. Is what happened really that important? Will it matter that much in a decade, or in a century? Will the course of the world be changed by it?

Recently a group of youths attacked a government official in Washington D. C. He was an innocent bystander to the main action, but in the attack he lost an eye. That could easily cause bitterness for years. But this man, a professing Christian, exhibited a remarkable spirit. He thanked God for giving him two eyes for 46 years, and he said if he was destined to live the rest of his life with one eye he would do so. He was free from any spirit of vengeance because of his relation to Christ. In a crisis situation, this man was true to his faith. He took a long-range, eternal view. There are things more important than losing an eye. It is worse to lose your values or convictions.

Resentment in Suffering

Third, let's learn a lesson from the cross. There is great value in unmerited suffering. Jesus did not deserve death. But he voluntarily accepted it for our sake. The way we react to wrongs we have suffered will influence others. For example, the influence of the man who lost one eye strengthened my faith.

We gain strength and depth in our relation to the Lord. He died, unjustly, praying for God to forgive his tormentors (Luke 23:34). If we are wronged, and bless rather than curse, we are linked with God like Jesus was. When we overcome resentment, we experience God's power in a special way. We grow through unmerited suffering. I'm not unsympathetic, but I believe we should thank God for suffering because it leads to spiritual progress.

Fourth, remember all of us have done wrong. Others have reason to resent us. We hope that they will also realize that love is not resentful.

Finally, we must reemphasize prayer. People may consider it impossible to forgive. But we must try. We should turn the matter over to God. We can ask him to help us. These attitudes do not change overnight, but they will eventually be changed by God's power.

Love is not resentful. What spirit could be more contrary to our Lord's life and mission? We must not let our lives contradict his by resenting, when he forgave.

11 THE JOYFUL SERVANT

The preacher in the Walt Disney movie *Pollyanna* was a hellfire and brimstone sort. He was so effective that some members of his congregation couldn't even eat Sunday dinner after he preached one of his "rip-snorters." Finally, Pollyanna reminded him that the Bible also includes many joy passages, and asked why he didn't preach on some of them. He was shocked, but not as shocked as the congregation was the first time he actually did preach a joy sermon. There they were, expecting another dose of sulphur, and out came a call to rejoice in the Lord.

Christianity is a joyful religion. Joy is at the very heart of it. God invented joy, and he intends to give it to his people. If they don't get it, they have missed much of what Christianity is about. After all, Jesus didn't come to make us miserable.

Gospel means good news, not bad news!

Paul says, "Love does not rejoice in wrong, but rejoices in the right." This gets to the center of Christian joy. It isn't a superficial "rah-rah" thing. We don't manufacture it out of our emotions. It drinks deeply from the heart of God.

Wrong has no real joy in it. And right cannot be separated from joy because God binds them together. There may be many wrong things that look like they can give joy and right things that look like they would produce misery. But both appearances are illusions. There is no real joy in wrong, and no right that is not joyous. God made things that way. Hell can't invent joy. It all comes from heaven.

When we live by joy, we are basically what God meant us to be. When we depart from it, we live a lie and rejoice where there is no real joy, which means our rejoicing is actually hollow.

Reacting to Wrong

Each of the terms we have discussed needs to be understood as it deals with interpersonal relationships. Wrong and right are broad terms, but Paul focuses in on wrong done by others. If I love people, I do not rejoice in their wrongs.

We see this idea more clearly by reading various translations of this passage. Moffatt says, "Love is never glad when others go wrong." Phillips says, "Love does not gloat over the wickedness of other people." The NEB translates it "Love does not gloat over other men's sins."

All the attributes discussed in previous chapters, including patience and freedom from resentment, deal with our own attitudes. They refer to what we should do regardless of how others act. But now the question is how we react to wrong in the lives

114

of others. Paul is thinking of any wrong someone else does, regardless of any prior sin we have committed. How will we act toward those who have gone astray?

Rejoicing in Faults

In the church in Corinth, many people rejoiced in the wrongs of others. They did little to solve their problems. If anything, they seem to have been aggravating them.

There was no sorrow over the man who was living immorally with his stepmother (5:2). The church, rather than withdrawing from immoral members, associated with people who were guilty of greed, idolatry, reveling, drunkenness, and robbery (5:9-11). Brethren hauled each other into court to be judged by pagans (6:1-8). They lacked sensitivity. The prevailing opinion seemed to be, "I'll do what I want. All things are lawful." Jealous and proud attitudes corrupted worship (chapters 10-16).

All of these matters should have grieved the church and called for action. But, to Paul's dismay, they were unchecked. Paul may have asked, "How can you rejoice when brethren are guilty of incest, arrogance, or jealousy?" And "rejoice" is not too strong a term because of two elements present at Corinth—competitiveness and carnality. These two combine to form jealousy, boastfulness and arrogance. It indicates to me that the brethren delighted in the mistakes and misdeeds of other Christians. The carnal people joined others who did wrong, and the competitive people delighted in the wrongs of their "enemies." The situation isn't unusual. You can find brethren today rejoicing at the wrongs of others.

Spiritual Smugness

We rejoice in the wrongs of others for several reasons. Their wrongdoing might bring us some advantage. Suppose we are in competition with another person. If he goes down, we go up. His mistakes benefit us. We are mainly concerned with what we can get out of it, not with the tragedy taking place in the other person's life (because they have sinned).

While we were children, my sisters and I frequently disagreed with each other. I often was glad when they did wrong and got caught because it made me look good, which suggests another reason we rejoice in the wrongs of others. We feel spiritually superior to them. We may not admit it, but most of us have expressed diabolical glee (no matter how slight) because we were better than someone else. The people who often criticized Jesus for his associations with sinners were "too good" to associate with tax collectors and prostitutes. Jesus, of course, cried out against spiritual smugness. He indicated that people whose "superiority" came at the expense of the faults of others were worse sinners than those they criticized.

We also rejoice in other's wrongs because of resentment. When they goof they get what they deserve, and they needn't come to us for sympathy. People smirk at the "fall" of a preacher, or notable person with whom they had a difference or a conflict.

Alone, we may be fairly discreet, but we are just waiting to be influenced. When another person takes the lead in doing wrong, we eagerly follow. Drinking, doping, swinging, or doing something illegal to make a few bucks—these have appeal to certain people at opportune times.

The Heart of the Gospel

But these kinds of rejoicing are far from the heart of the gospel. The incarnation took place because of God's love for his rebellious creatures. He loved them so much that he became flesh. As he approached Jerusalem, Jesus shook with sobs (Luke 19:41). He did so, I think, because the city was the center of Jewish rejection of God's son. God cares so much that we *not* sin that he has done everything for us short of forcing us to obey him against our wills.

If I rejoice in the wrongs of others, I contradict God's purpose for making, sustaining and redeeming us. I violate the entire holy history which he directed through the ages of man. I leave the path that led Jesus to the cross.

In a sense, rejoicing in wrong casts a vote for a universe where evil, not good, rules men's lives. Of course, none of us would admit casting that vote. But our attitudes may be leading us in that direction. Jesus died to defeat evil. How can we find joy when evil wins in someone else's life?

Joy in Salvation

God calls us to serve, not to pursue life selfishly. The greatest way to serve is to help deliver someone from Satan's control. But how can I do that for a person if I rejoice in his faults? I can help him find a right relationship with God only when I am as grieved about his wrongs as I am for my own. Do I want the other person to move closer to God or farther from him? Do I want him to benefit from Christ's death and resurrection? Am I happy when another person is destroyed? If I am, how could my attitude even remotely reflect the mind of Christ?

Now turn this around. How would you feel if you knew others were rejoicing in your wrongdoing? Do you want people to hope you wander further away from God rather than closer to him? "How could others be so callous and uncaring toward me when I sin?" And reverse the question: "How can I be so unloving when others sin?"

In the beatitudes, Jesus blessed people who mourn. He says people who mourn over the sins of humanity are truly happy. They find comfort in knowing the power of redemption. Jesus calls his people to grieve over the wrongs of others. They should dedicate themselves to easing the problem of human sinfulness by doing all they can to deliver others from the power of sin. This includes evangelism and edification. This concern should be the very heart of our faith. It is the very meaning of Christianity. Paul's statement is far more important than we might realize. He calls us away from preoccupation with self to the broader life of service, which is a demonstration of the mind of Christ.

Rejoicing in the Right

Paul also says, "Love rejoices in the right." Right refers to something which is unchangeable and reliable. Of course, a person could be unchangeably and reliably bad. But the root meaning of the word rules that out. The idea refers to something which remains the same even when everything else changes, and something which is reliable even if everything else is unreliable. Paul says love rejoices in that which is steadfast, dependable, constant, etc. So we see that love rejoices in God, upon whom we can absolutely depend. All joy in right is really joy in God himself.

Since love deals with human relations, Paul means we should be glad when men put on God's nature and live it out in their lives. This is the greatest human experience of all. If we don't find joy here, then our whole idea of rejoicing is probably warped.

To rejoice in right is to rejoice when men are drawn to Christ (evangelism). To rejoice in right is to rejoice when the church extends God's love to people in need (benevolence). To rejoice in right is to find joy when Christians are strengthened and when they strengthen each other (edification). It is to rejoice in virtue. It is to rejoice in victory over sin. It is to rejoice in interpersonal relations strengthened by the love of God. It is to rejoice when people are reunited. It is to rejoice when church divisions are healed. It is to rejoice when Christians improve their relation to God. It is to rejoice when people overcome enslaving habits. We rejoice in seeing men become more like their Maker and Redeemer.

Moral actions are more significant than simply keeping or breaking "laws." They tell us how to be godlike. Loving people rejoice to see the kingdom of God increase and to see more and more people place themselves under the sovereignty of the Lord. God's love leads us to this goal. His love works in us to help others, giving us a part in fulfilling his purposes for humanity!

12 THE ENDURING PROOF

The subject of love is endless, and the practice of love is never fully achieved. It relates to every part of life. The general outline of this book follows Paul's writing in 1 Corinthians 13:1-7. He completes his list of love's characteristics with four statements which tell us that love "bears," "believes," "hopes," and "endures" "all things."

Love bears all things. What does it mean? The root meaning of bears (Greek *stegō*) is to cover. There are two possible applications. First, it can mean to "cover" something with silence, keep it secret, or hide and conceal it. The Moffatt translation adopts this meaning: "Love is always slow to expose" (1 Corinthians 13:7). Love is slow to expose the errors or faults of others.

Second, it may mean love can bear up, hold out against, endure, or forbear threatening circumstances.

Even though the second meaning is most often accepted, the first also deserves our attention. Love covers and hides the sins of others. This doesn't mean we should ignore wrong or deny it serious consideration. It does mean a loving person recognizes that advertising the sins of others publicly may not be the best way to help them overcome their sins. This idea closely relates to not rejoicing in wrong (chapter 11). You can probably think of many times when wrongs of others have been made public. You might also remember being suspicious of the motives and wondering if it caused more harm than good. Sometimes people expose others only to feel self-righteous. They have very little, if any, desire to help the sinner.

'Did you hear about . . . ?'

Gossip is perhaps more devastating. Some of it is malicious and some innocent. It can be harmful in either case. You've heard these before. "Did you hear about . . . ?" Or, "I know this won't go any further, so I can tell you." We often get into these conversations because we can't think of anything else to say. However, at other times our motives are much less innocent. Remember, the harm is done when the words are said, regardless of why. The ideal, of course, is to first think about other people and the possible effect of our words on them. We should keep our mouths closed, or talk about other things. Silence will not destroy us, but unkind words may well destroy someone else.

To be true to our Christian calling, there are times when we dare not "cover" wrongdoing. For example, Paul vigorously and openly names sins and sinners and opposes wrong (1 Cor. 5:1-5). It was shameful for a man to be living with his

122

father's wife. The time had come for sin to be openly identified. The wrong may have already been widely known and brought reproach upon the church. It had to be dealt with publicly. But Paul carefully noted in the biblical context that he first considered the salvation of the offenders.

Paul also instructs Timothy (1 Tim. 5:20) about people who persist in sin. They are to be rebuked before all. This passage could easily be misused by unloving people to justify uncharitable denunciations of brothers in Christ. But we must suppose, considering New Testament teaching, that Paul's main concern was not just to expose sin, but to save sinners. At times, exposure seems the only mode of redemptive action possible. When those times come, it must be done.

Help or Hurt?

Elders sometimes find it necessary to publicize sin within the congregation. Requests are received about preachers who want to relocate, and honesty sometimes demands that unattractive facts be revealed. The acid test is whether these revelations are designed to help or hurt the concerned individual. The same principles apply in similar situations outside the church. A Christian operating in the "secular" world will also want love to control his public assessments of others.

In summary, it is best not to spread knowledge of the sins of others. But if scripture or circumstances demand that something be said, then we must very carefully examine our motives so that everything is done in the loving spirit of Jesus.

Some people argue that if you don't expose a person's sin, you are just as guilty as he is. They believe it is dishonest to hide a sin, and it may even imply some moral softness. They assume that if you don't condemn the sin, you endorse it. Someone once accused me of agreeing with all the positions endorsed by a certain controversial magazine because I once published an article in the magazine without condemning their "errors." The article was simply a review of some commentaries on an Old Testament book! It seems to me that it isn't practical or logical to expect a book review to examine the entire editorial policy of a paper. We are all associated with people whose ideas we would not accept (school, work, neighborhoods, organizations). That doesn't imply either our endorsement or moral softness. We simply can't spend all of our time talking about what we think is wrong about the PTA or the office staff, or even the members of the church.

Paul didn't think public exposure of sin was always appropriate. After all, God knows what we do wrong, and usually we do too.

Holding Out Against It All

"To bear" also means to endure, forbear, or hold out against anything. This is the modern meaning of the word. The same Greek term in 1 Corinthians 9:12 expresses Paul's willingness to bear anything, rather than put an obstacle in the way of the gospel. He speaks of his personal decision not to accept support for his preaching, though he argued he had the right to receive it. He had resolved to "bear" whatever difficulties and inconveniences were involved in supporting himself because he felt it was best for his ministry.

The only other place the term for "bear" is used in the New Testament is 1 Thessalonians 3:1, 5. On his second mission tour Paul went from Berea to

Athens. Timothy joined him in Athens. We suppose, from his writings at the time, that he was disheartened and deeply in need of Timothy's companionship. But he was also extremely concerned about the Thessalonian Christians. Finally, he could bear his concern for their welfare no more. He sent Timothy to learn of their faith "for fear that somehow the tempter had tempted you and that our labor would be in vain." He knew his own loneliness, frustration, discouragement, and other problems would be intensified without Timothy. But he was willing to "bear" them because he wanted to know about his brethren in Thessalonica.

Since love is concerned with relations between people, "all things" deals also with people rather than circumstances. We must learn to hate the sin, but love the sinner (and never get the two confused). Love for individuals should continue, no matter how perverse they become. Paul took this position toward his Corinthian brethren, judging from the wrongs described in First Corinthians and from Paul's loving appeals to them to return to the Lord. Christians should learn to endure each other so that neither injury, insult, nor disappointment will damage proper Christian concerns for one another.

Fruit of Intolerance

Notice how frequently the Corinthians neglected this. Had they borne all things, they would not have been characterized by quarreling and factionalism (1 Cor. 1:11). Dispute and disagreement are not necessarily wrong in themselves. But often they are done with the wrong spirit, as in Corinth. They were jealous of others who claimed superior status or blessings (3:3). Some were puffed up against others (4:6). Some were not willing to bear weak brethren in the matter of food (8:12). Loving people would have endured weak brothers and voluntarily abstained from things which were morally offensive.

Perhaps the best illustration is Paul's discussion of brethren going to law with one another. Rather than accept wrongs done to them, brothers went to court with each other before judges who did not believe in Christ. Paul told the Corinthians that they would really lose, even if their legal cases were victorious, because loving relations between brethren would be destroyed. I believe Paul was less concerned about the use of the legal process than about the wrong attitudes characterizing those who used it. There are certain rights a Christian legitimately claims, and he might use legal procedures to preserve them. In some cases, it might even be wrong to keep an offender from facing up to the legal implications of his act. But when people use the legal process with an unloving vindictive spirit, then they refuse to "bear all things." Our greatest right is to love God, and thus to love his creatures. Nothing should cause us to violate that.

Paul tells Christians that loving endurance is the key to avoiding quarreling, jealousy, boasting, and partisanship. We must learn to live with our brothers and help them. Some may not fit our mold. But love rises above insisting that other people conform to our opinions. We can have this love if we realize that our stability does not depend on our own opinions, or on fallible humans. It depends upon the changeless Christ, who is the same yesterday, today, and forever. We draw strength from this rock-like resource.

Love Believes All Things

Love's qualities of believing, hoping, and enduring are closely related. If I believe in God, that faith gives me hope. If I believe in man, I hope for man's improvement. Hope is often associated with endurance. I will endure whatever is necessary to reach an important goal. The Christian should consider final fellowship with God of such overpowering importance that he lets nothing keep him from attaining it.

What does love believe *in*? What is the object of love's belief? We need to consider two answers, one in this chapter and one in the next. First, love believes God. Second, love believes in man. You probably think more about love for man since love is a social thing. But Paul may be talking here about belief in God. The strength of my faith in God controls the depth of my faith in man. Trusting in God gives me a foundation that makes love for others possible.

It isn't always easy to believe in God and his promises. We are often so selfish that we refuse to trust him. We should recall the mass of testimony telling us that his promises have been fulfilled. A good example is Hebrews 11, with its roll call of heroes of faith. These verses tell us that God always comes through as he promises. He is the one absolutely dependable factor in all the universe.

Believe Also in Others

If we believe in God, we are free to give our love to others. We believe that we are truly forgiven by the blood of Christ. Since he has forgiven us, we are free from worry about our relation to God. We no longer need to try to earn his forgiveness. We do not need to feel guilty for sins he has already taken away. We should quit trying to be saved solely by our own efforts and accept the gift of Jesus' saving blood.

We believe his promise to show us, in every temptation, a way of escape (1 Cor. 10:13). We know a divine aid complements our feeble efforts. Thus we can live more confidently. We have help from beyond. We have joy in that knowledge.

We believe he will answer prayers, as he promised (Luke 11:1-13). We believe he will give strength in trial (Acts 4:23-31). We believe he will give wisdom (James 1:5). We believe he will guide his people as they do his will. We believe he will bless his work, and that he will give the eventual victory.

It is easy to become disheartened. It seems like we will never correct the problems of the church. We simply cannot lead people to Christ. They are not interested. No sooner have we converted a number of people than they move away. We think God doesn't realize how severe our problems are. We need to be optimistic and recognize that all things, under God, will finally turn out for the best. Success will come in God's work. God cannot fail or be defeated. We need to believe that improvement is possible, even today. By faith we need to dare great things.

Faith and Failure

We must also be realistic. We must not assume that God always intends to accomplish his purposes through some particular method or scheme that we have devised. Our plan may be flawed. God may need to teach us a better way by allowing us to fail. But this does not mean God fails. It only indicates the inadequacy of a human scheme to accomplish his purposes. With ultimate faith in his power, we need to adopt another plan or method, and then move forward.

God certainly wants men and women to find life's fullest meaning by coming to Christ. There are many methods for bringing people to the Lord. They include visual aids, scripture tracts, door-to-door canvassing, campaigns, records, correspondence courses, and soul talks. Some methods are appropriate for some people and not for others. If one procedure fails, does that prove God is no longer concerned with soul winning? Of course not! He is simply telling us to try another approach. His love remains constant, even if our methods must change.

Many interpersonal problems are probably caused because men lack inner peace that comes from a proper relationship with God. So the greater our faith in him, the greater the love and concern we can show for others. Faith in God also leads to faith in others.

13 THE LOVE DECISION

Love maintains a "high" view of human nature. It affirms the good about man. Love allows for circumstances and sees the best in others. It sees potential in people and the good they already possess, not just their present evil. But don't misunderstand me. We are sinners, constitutionally unable to do God's will as we ought. Every one of us, save the Lord, makes mistakes. I do not believe man is essentially good. I believe he is essentially a sinner. That is the whole point of the story of the fall (Gen. 3) and of the rest of the biblical story.

But I also believe man is improvable. This is accomplished by the grace of God. Some day, praise God, we will be free from sinful tendencies. Until then, we are transgressors whom God must continually deliver and elevate. So when I speak of affirming the good about man, I mean we must have willingness to be charitable in our judgments and take into account God's work in transforming lives.

C. S. Lewis pictures heaven as a place of ever increasing closeness to God. There are always greater heights to be ascended, greater joys to be known. We must not lose sight of our potential to be drawn closer to God. God never wants us to move away from him. Even when we stand still we invite stagnation. And that also increases our distance from God.

So those "lovers" who "believe all things" share the wish and expectation that men can move toward God. We were made for this. This is how we ought to feel toward those who have wronged us: "You may have cursed me, cheated me, lied about me, or slandered me, but you can be better. I still believe in you, and I'll help you improve."

Belief by Association

God changes the lives of many people through some other person who "believed all things" about them. It means so much to find someone who has faith in us and who will not give up on us, no matter how bad we are. Believing all things about someone we can influence may make the difference between their salvation or damnation. A husband (or wife) becomes a better person because of the faith of the mate. A child, in times of difficulty, finds parents who believe in him, and through this faith he comes through the trials to be an outstanding human being. Juvenile delinquents are rescued by wise counselors who have faith in their improvability.

If I believe in my fellow man, I will encourage him. I will forgive him. I will try to understand him. I will assist him. I will try to help him find the meaning in life only Christ can give. If I do not believe in him, I will belittle him. I will criticize him. I will mistreat him. I will refuse to forgive him. I will resent him. And I will certainly not try to convert him. If I believe in him, I will not downgrade him before others. If I don't believe in him, who knows what I might say about him.

Examine how you treat others for a week. Don't do it superficially. Think about as many relationships as you can, and analyze each one carefully. You will soon know whether or not you believe in others.

There is a problem involved in this optimistic attitude toward others. If we have confidence in others, someone will surely take advantage of us. Some people will manipulate the goodness of others to their own gain. That's part of the problem of living among a fallen race.

The Risk of Believing

So what will we lose if someone does take advantage of us? Some pride, possibly. And likely something material. And perhaps some peace of mind. Now we can solve this problem by shutting off our trusting love. That way we can be suspicious, even paranoid, defensive, and closed. But this is too high a price to pay. We lose more than we gain.

Is it such a great risk to believe all things when we consider the possible gains? Isn't love always taking risks? Doesn't it gain its great rewards at the chance of being hurt? We really can't find genuine happiness without involvement, and involvement may open us up to pain.

Think about Jesus. He never pulled his love

back. He continued to give it with a burning intensity even though giving it often caused him suffering. He made himself vulnerable, and some of his enemies attacked him in what seemed to be his areas of vulnerability. But he refused to abandon his mission. He remained open and loving. He continued to take chances until he was finally spiked to the cross. Surely he could have chosen not to be crucified. He could have decided not to go to Jerusalem, or even fled from Gethsemane before his captors arrived. But that would have been inconsistent with his love for humanity. He suffered for a greater good.

When we look at Jesus, knowing that he was raised and that he now lives at God's right hand, we learn something about his "weakness." He was not really weak at all. But his source of strength was so different from our conception of it that he appeared defenseless. His strength was the very strength of God himself—of the God who gives meaning to the word strength. So rather than withdraw because we are selfishly afraid we will be hurt, we should take the risk to believe in people and selflessly offer ourselves for their good. Even if someone occasionally takes advantage of us, it probably won't kill us (though it killed Jesus). It's better to know we have lived lovingly and to rely on the unending power of God to see us through. I would rather lose a few dollars, or some of my pride, than lose my relation to God by not "believing all things."

The Good Sense Quotient

Paul certainly does not intend for us to be the gullible dupes of every rogue. If our suspicions about someone are justified, we can take appropriate action motivated by love. We don't give up believing in what the person might be. Many ministers have been approached by what might be called the "professional religious vagrant." They travel across the country, going from church to church, begging for handouts. Some have done it for so long they have refined their "stories" over and over to cover all the loopholes. After listening for an hour, any reason you might have for saying "no" is answered. These people have learned a sort of religious blackmail. They are masters at playing on feelings of pity and guilt. But very often they might use whatever money is given them to pursue destructive habits. They might be alcoholics or drug users, begging to support their habit. Many ministers and elders, therefore, refuse to give money to such people. But they readily offer to give them food, lodging, clothes, or gasoline. That way a need, if genuine, is met, but the generosity is tempered with good sense. They don't encourage bad habits. They are concerned that these "vagrants" might find a better way of life through God's grace.

Look also at a teacher's attitude toward students who are suspected of cheating on examinations. The class could follow an honor system, but it might be misused. So the teacher takes certain precautions to insure that honest work is done. At the same time, the teacher hopes that the students examine their own value systems and learn the worth of honesty as a rule of life. This approach combines good sense and trust. It is a loving way to deal with the problem.

The Picture of Glory

The New Testament draws a thrilling picture of the glory promised to Christians. In fact, we are experiencing the beginning of it now. In 2 Corinthians 3:18, Paul says we are changed from glory to glory. In Romans 8:29, he says we shall have a body like the glorious body of Christ. He also pictures the exalted nature of the spiritual body in 1 Corinthians 15:42-44, 49-54. These marvelous passages describe our potentiality. I am more than delighted at this prospect for my life. I can be like the Lord, shining with a glory beyond my most exalted imagination. I realize that same glory is possible for anyone who will be God's person. I want to see people that way. I want to rivet my attention on what they can become—what I hope they will become. I want to keep in mind the glorious destiny for which God has intended them. It isn't always easy to think that way. My own ego, as well as interpersonal difficulties, get in the way. It must have been hard for the Corinthians to have such a viewpoint. Yet all things are possible with God.

By proper attitudes we stay firm and calm. As a result, we can be a constant source of strength to others. We can have a love that believes all things because of the one upon whom our faith is founded. Surely other people should act the right way. But even if they don't, our love can overcome their inadequacy.

Much of what we have said about "believes all things" involves hope because it is centered in the expectations we have for others. Much of the following discussions of "endures all things" also talks about hope. Paul focuses on a hope centered in what people can become.

Reaching the Destination

Students of the Bible sometimes can't distinguish between the meanings of "bears all things" and "endures all things." "Endures" seems to imply a period of time more than "bears" does. "Bears all things" does indicate a loving attitude must be exhibited as long as a problem exists. But "endures" implies a long-time perseverance and patience. Some suggest that "bears" describes the initial attitude toward another person, while "endures" describes the continuation of that attitude. "Bears" is like starting the car and leaving the driveway, while "endures" is like driving all the way to the destination.

The verb for endures is *hupomenō*. One meaning is "to remain." Another is "to wait" for someone. But most of the references indicate patience, steadfastness, or endurance, all of which imply a long-term outlook. In the New Testament, the word is commonly used with tribulation. Suffering produces endurance, which eventually produces hope (Rom. 5:3). The Thessalonians were commended for their steadfastness in the face of the afflictions they were enduring (2 Thess. 1:4). The book of Revelation speaks frequently of the endurance of the saints in the presence of persecution (Rev. 1:9; 3:10; 13:10).

The term is also connected with faith, which produces steadfastness (James 1:3). There is also joy in the exercise of patience (Col. 1:11). And hope comes in connection with steadfastness (Rom. 5:3; 15:4f.; 1 Thess. 1:3). Most often the idea of patient hope is found in passages indicating the goal of glory that challenges the Christian (Luke 21:19; Rom. 2:7; 2 Tim. 2:10, 12; Heb.

10:36; 12:2; James 1:12; 5:11). Barclay says that *hupomonē* is not passive. It indicates the spirit that endures with a blazing hope because it knows glory awaits. It does not grimly wait for the end, but hopes for the dawn. It cannot be injured by human power or by evil force. It changes the hardest trial into glory because beyond the pain it sees the goal. It is an active, positive fortitude. It refuses to be overwhelmed, but holds on in spite of any difficulty.

Fighting Back with God's Power

Endurance is essential to the Christian because he is in a world where opposing forces continue to rage against his faith. But remember that Paul was most concerned with how the Corinthians treated each other. He wanted them to develop an enduring hope for one another. He may imply that men who share the same hope of ultimate unity with God dare not defy that hope by being divided upon earth. If we hope for the salvation of others, and of ourselves, that has a profound influence on how we treat those others. Many of the things done in Corinth certainly failed to promote the hope of other Christians for glory. The attitudes and practices were hellish, not heavenly. If Christians live in the mutual hope of glory, then endurance is necessary each day. Rather than opposing and giving up on each other, we need to patiently apply God's power to current problems. The Corinthians needed to work toward resolution. So do we. And they needed to recognize that solutions sometimes come slowly (from human perspectives). So do we.

Christians should not give up just because the situation among the saints appears grim and discouraging. There are always problems on the road of faith. Many of them attack our emotions in ways that are hard to understand. Satan will tempt us in every conceivable way. But we must have endurance and loving commitment to the ideal of service to others. Only there will we find victory. Whatever the obstacles may be, it is always preferable to persevere in love than to react with hatred, bitterness, cynicism, or apathy.

Enduring the Mission

Because of unhappiness, some people abandon any relationship with the church. Often they retain a faith in Christ, but refuse involvement with other Christians. Others totally abandon any relation to Jesus and replace it with bitterness and cynicism. They become disillusioned with others, or become disappointed with the way they have been treated or with the hypocrisy within the church. But what are their priorities? Must we insist that the people in the church satisfy us? Are we responsible for the whole church? Rather, aren't we called to have a patient love for the brothers, no matter what happens around us? Is not the whole idea of Christianity to be givers because so much has been given to us?

We must endure because we are loving. We can help someone. Our abdication does not help answer the needs within the church. It does not help improve the very problems that we find so irritating. Aren't we really selfish if we quit simply because people don't do things our way? Doesn't God need people who are working patiently and lovingly to bring us all nearer to him?

Jesus endured mental pressure; the horrible anticipation of the passion, plotting, and misunderstanding by those closest him; betrayal of a close disciple; pain (beatings, thorns, a cross); mockery, the worst sort of slander and insult; and a terrible sense of desolation while on the cross. But his love endured all things. What would it mean for us if his love had not endured? Is not our mission to follow him? The next time we are tempted to quit loving others because of what they have done, we need to remember Jesus.

The Greatest of These . . .

Faith and hope will not abide as love abides. Faith and hope are man's responses to God. They will be less necessary as we approach perfection. They will eventually be transcended when the object of our faith will be known and our hope realized. But not so with love. It is the very nature of heaven and of the God who makes heaven by his presence. This will be our glory. There all will be giving, and receiving, and giving again. All selfishness will disappear. Gone will be impatience, unkindness, jealousy, boastfulness, arrogance, rudeness, irritability, resentment, and rejoicing in wrong. From our earthly perspective it is impossible for us to understand the fullness of that love. It lies beyond us, but we are growing toward it daily as we live here on earth. We progress, and over the years the vision becomes a bit more clear. One day it will burst upon us in all its glory. Then we will know it was for this we were made, and will see that many things which seemed important on earth had really worked against our glory.

It all comes back to what we put first in our lives—self or God. From this most elemental of equations flows all that we have tried to say in these pages.

Journey
Adult Bible Studies

An entire series of resources for group or personal adult study.

Other titles include:

OUR LIFE TOGETHER by James Thompson
> This best-selling book offers a fresh look at Christian fellowship. (JA101S)

CHOSEN FOR RICHES by Bob Hendren
> A life-related exposition of Ephesians (JA102S)

WHAT EVERY FAMILY NEEDS or **WHATEVER HAPPENED TO MOM, DAD, AND THE KIDS?** by Paul Faulkner and Carl Breechen
> Explore biblical principles for healthy family life (JA103S)

WHO RULES YOUR LIFE? by Prentice Meador
> Explore the kingdom parables of Jesus (JA104S)

THE POWER TO BE by Tom Olbricht
> The life style of Jesus from Mark's gospel (JA105S)

STRATEGY FOR SURVIVAL by James Thompson
> A plan for church renewal from Hebrews (JA106S)

All of the above paperbacks are supported by a **Journeys Teacher's Manual/Resource Kit,** containing 13 practical lesson plans for weekly Bible study (lecture and group discussion), two-color overhead transparencies and Explorer sheets on duplicator masters.

TO ORDER: Contact your local religious bookstore or call toll-free, **1-800-531-5220 (U.S.) or 1-800-252-9213 (TX)**